Other Books By Heather Christie

THE
LYING
SEASON

L♥VE NOTES!

Real Stories. Real People. Real Love.

SELECTED AND CREATED BY HEATHER CHRISTIE, EDITOR

LOVENOTES!

Real Stories.

Real People.

Real Love.

***Spreading love
one story at a time.***

Heather Christie

**71st
Street
BOOKS
NEW YORK**

www.71streetbooks.com

LOVENOTES!
Real Stories. Real People. Real Love.

Selected and Created by Heather Christie, Editor

Published by 71 Street Books, New York

Copyright © 2024

All rights reserved.

Though this is a collection of true stories, some names of people and places have been changed in the spirit of privacy and protection.

979-8-9917047-2-4 (softcover)

979-8-9917047-7-9 (hardback)

979-8-9917047-1-7 (e-book)

It's all for you—Cole & Cali

LOVE NOTES!

Real People. Real Stories. Real Love.

America's Best Love Stories & More!

Selected & Created by

Heather Christie

Editor

"All You Need Is Love"

JOHN LENNON

A LOVE NOTE

From the Editor

Dear Reader,

It's the dinner hour when the ghosts show no mercy. That's why before I leave my New York City flat, I stage it, making sure there are fresh flowers on the dining table, that my corner lamp is set to dim, and Alexa has my favorite indie folk channel playing. I'm lucky—my apartment faces southeast and is filled with natural light and positive energy. It's where I've rebuilt my life and it's unapologetically decorated in bright orange, hot pink, and navy blue. There are no remnants from my life before, only the photos of my children. Each morning I smile at my living room, and then I head out for the day.

Evening after evening, when I return home, I push open my apartment door and there's a moment when my trick has worked—the place feels alive. I believe I am not alone. That my partner has arrived home first. Maybe he's in the kitchen preparing our evening meal or taking a shower after a long day's work. It's in this witching hour that I ache for the rhythm of a family unit, for the life I thought I was supposed to have, for the love that somehow missed me.

When I was nineteen years old, I traded in my show business dreams and left New York City after a six-month, hormone-fueled, whirlwind courtship to marry a professional soccer player under the pressure of my parents, who were loving and kind but carried the orthodox expectations of traditional Europe. In the years that followed, I gave birth to two children: Cole and Cali—the most beautiful gifts of my life—and because of them, I tried harder and harder to make my marriage work. That's what a good wife, a good mother does, right? She keeps her family together, even if it means losing herself. Maybe it was the happy example of my parents' fifty-three-year wedlock that kept me thinking my marriage was just about to get better if I gave it a little more time.

Flash forward twenty-nine years, when I finally conceded that my happily-ever-after wasn't happening. My marriage ultimately buckled under the weight of our incompatibility and my ex-husband's addictions. At age forty-nine, two weeks into Covid, I filed for divorce and moved in with my mother. A year later, my kids launched, and carrying the broken pieces of my life, I returned to New York City to begin again. I was somehow convinced that true love was just around the corner. All I had to do was sign up for Bumble and my Prince Charming would miraculously appear. Well, many, many first dates later—I'm as single as single can be!

Now, date ##? almost did me in for good. We'd arranged to meet at the Dakota Bar, a well-known watering hole on Seventy-second Street near my house. Oh jeez, he was an obnoxious New Jersey lawyer (not there's anything wrong with lawyers or New Jersey), but this man was much older and much heavier than his profile picture; worse though, he was a misogynist and racist. The final straw was when he said he wanted to read his novel-in-progress to me later that evening—*naked*. I waved for the check.

"What are you doing?" he asked, surprised.

"I'm calling *this* right now." My inner (unbeknownst-to-me) badass diva took over and I smacked my American Express card on the bar, paid for the two unfinished drinks, and escaped into the Dakota's bathroom. My heart pounded and my hands shook, and I deleted every dating app on my phone. Done. Done. Done.

The adrenaline was soaring through my body when I stopped at the deli to buy flowers. My arms were full of roses (I was celebrating my girl power move), when I dropped my phone on the sidewalk. As I rose, the most gorgeous, red-headed, young Irish man was standing in front of me, like he'd just stepped out of a storybook.

"I almost got hit by a car crossing the street. I found 'ya so distracting me." He smiled, his green eyes twinkling. "I had to turn around and take a chance ya'd speak with me."

No kidding. This happened. Like a scene in a romantic comedy on the big screen. And so we exchanged numbers, and we went on a couple of dates, until I cyberstalked him on LinkedIn and learned he was really decades younger than me and that was probably not going to work.

But the young Irish gent was enough of a nudge from the universe—a little "don't give up quite yet, Heather." Anything can happen. Even in New York City, where fast-paced pedestrians don't make eye contact with each other, you might just bump into someone.

So I carried on. And then finally, finally, finally he appeared. THE ONE. A soulful, soccer-playing musician, with deep brown eyes, a mane of hair, and a connection that felt true and pure. It was as if every wrong turn I'd ever taken now made sense; each misstep had been leading me to him. I could see the future and it was so bright.

There was one problem.

My ONE had no idea I was *HIS* one. And as fast as he came into my life, he hightailed it through the Lincoln Tunnel, never to be seen in these parts again. Can you say *heartbroken*?

Eighteen months of therapy later, I was finally ready to brave the dating scene once more. Clad in my skin-tight, black leather jeans (the stretchy kind) and sexy cutout turtleneck, I pulled myself up by my heart-strings and headed straight to Tantra speed dating—a mindful, intentional way of connecting—at least that's what their website said.

I met a guy who checked every box: enlightened, smart, handsome, and so on. All systems fired, saying *it's time to give the new fella a chance.*

The mindful dude and I went on a few very long dates—the chemistry was sizzling and he was doing everything right. I was imagining all sorts of future possibilities—you can fill in the blanks of my fairy-tale ride into the sunset.

We were texting one night when, in midconversation—a communication I might add that the mindful bozo had initiated—he vanished into thin air, gone like the wind. Maybe something tragic happened, you ask? Trust me, the ghost is alive and still haunts the Earth, able-bodied and apparently in good humor. Remember, I am a cyber sleuth.

But the ambassador of love can't give up, can she? I guess it's time for me to fire up Bumble again. Unless you want to set me up with a charming, single, middle-aged gentleman? You have permission to share my photo and email address ;-).

Joking aside, I know it's all going to work out in the end. The divine plan will be revealed. My great-grandmother, Albina, was a mail-order bride. As a young Polish girl, she sailed across the Atlantic Ocean, leaving the only family and home she'd ever known. She landed at Ellis Island in December, just a few miles from where I live now. Only nineteen years old, alone and speaking no English, I'm sure she was cold and frightened. She waited and waited, in this foreign land for her soon-to-be husband and for the life she was about to begin. My guess is she was doing a bit of that fantastical futurizing I am so guilty of.

The chap never showed up.

Talk about a ghosting of epic proportions. The family lore is sketchy and I am not sure how she ended up in the coal region of Pennsylvania. But my great-grandmother survived and if she hadn't been abandoned, *I wouldn't be here.*

May I honor her and the mysterious and magical ways love finds where it is supposed to land. The universe keeps nudging me—just look around, find the evidence. And, violá! Here I am—the creator of Love-Notes! (this book, the off-Broadway show, the satellite shows, and the soon-to-be-launched podcast). While I may not have stumbled upon my true love (yet), these stories of first love, last love, and all the messy love in between are pretty solid proof that it exists.

If you're happily coupled—thank you for reading and congratulations. But I want to give an especially warm welcome to the broken-hearted readers, the ones who've given up on love, the people who've lost hope—grab your cup of tea and cozy up on the sofa. My friends, this book is for us—for *you and me.*

I'm grateful for it all: the pain, the heartbreak, the reckoning of the life I didn't get; my precious children, my loyal family, and my deep friendships; but most of all at this moment in time, I am grateful for the hope that this book represents.

May we all find our person.

Here's looking for YOU—my *last* first date. I'm leaving the lights on so you can find your way home.

Xoxo,

Heather Christie

LoveNotes! Creator & Editor

P.S. I got a dog to keep me company in the meantime.

"First love is like a sunrise - it awakens your heart to a world of possibilities."

UNKNOWN

PLAYGROUND

Avis Yarbrough

Our eyes were trained on the seventh-grade boys. We'd done this before, and when the right moment arrived, we struck, sprinting to the green gate where their coats hung to snag them. Virginia took Aaron's black jacket and I took David's green coat. Safely on the other side of the playground, we smiled at each other in triumph. They were too busy playing football to notice it was winter in Chicago, freezing cold, and so bitter that we shivered against the blistering wind in our down-filled ski jackets. Snowflakes drifted from the darkened sky. Those boys were going to miss their coats, and we didn't feel bad.

We were nine years old and we knew our own hearts. Virginia loved Aaron and David was mine. My David was gorgeous, with his light brown skin and intense brown eyes. He hadn't known me until I started stealing his coat at recess, and I was going to make sure he would never forget me. All is fair in love and war.

We have their coats. We have their coats. Yay! I chanted in my head. And without guilt, we kept them the whole recess. Virginia was bold and, tempting fate, carried their jackets to her class. It is one thing to snatch coats, but another to keep them. This was big. Back in math class, my teacher was reviewing a lesson and I was writing down what she wrote on the board when the class door crashed open.

"They are after us! They know and they're pissed." It was Virginia, coats in hand. Her black hair was in disarray and her eyes wild. She ranted, but her nonsensical jabber made perfect sense to me. We were in huge love trouble.

My teacher calmly turned to Virginia. "Do you have a hall pass?"

Virginia took off. My classmates, astonished by the intrusion, watched me dash after her. In the school hallway, I caught up with her just as Aaron stormed around the corner.

"Oh, God," I said, gasping for air and hoping David was with him. I wished I had a mirror to make sure I looked good.

"Do you have our coats?" Aaron scowled pure venom.

It was obvious he was sick of both of us. But where was David?

Virginia sheepishly handed over the confiscated coats. Aaron said something to Virginia (lucky girl), but I wasn't interested. He was not my beloved. I returned to class upset that David had sent Aaron to retrieve his coat. Didn't he want to see me?

I could have denied I had the coat, which would have been true and might have lured David. Was David a wimp? Didn't he have the courage to confront me? No. No. He must have been too overcome with romantic emotion to face me, realizing he wouldn't be able to contain his strong feelings. *Oh, that is so sweet*, I thought. My beloved David.

The rest of the day was uneventful. My teacher was not fazed by the antics of lovesick, nine-year-old girls stealing indifferent, eleven-year-old boys' coats. When the school bell rang, Virginia and I strolled down Wabash Street together.

"Dibs," I said, seeing a red Porsche that I wanted when I turned sixteen.

Virginia countered with takers on a black Corvette. We laughed and smiled. Both of us were in a good mood.

We were in love and nothing could get us down.

FIRST LOVE = A MAZE

Follow your heart!

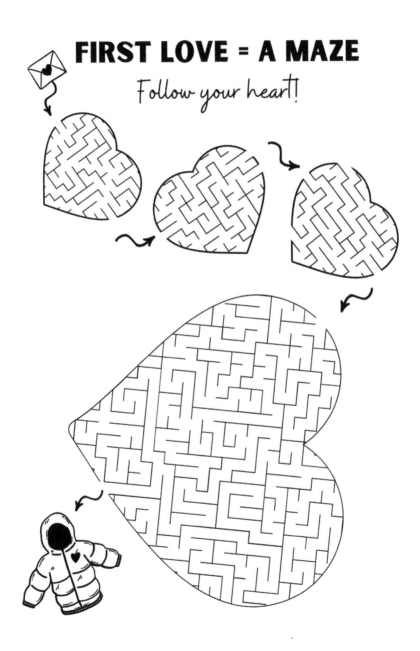

FIRST LOVE

Sunny Laprade

First love. For me, it was a classic story. We hated each other!

Her name was Emily. We had known each other since preschool and we'd been enemies the whole time, exchanging pointed and personal jabs every morning on the school bus and even nastier little quips during lunch, before our puberty-fueled hunger had been sated. But, as we both stumbled clumsily into adolescence and with it sexual maturity, or more accurately sexual immaturity, something changed.

By tenth grade, we were each fifteen; she had grown to a staggering six feet tall, which was nothing in comparison to my gargantuan five foot five. Our dynamic had aged like vinegar, only getting nastier and more acidic with time. At some point that old adage began to creep in, "They're only mean because they like you." Apparently our peers picked up on the tension between us, because that year we were voted Spirit Week Prince and Princess, which Emily was predictably quite angry about, her face turning bright red, the color of love.

Not long after that I asked her out, on the bus ride home, of course. We went to the one coffee shop in our tiny town, and I, ever the romantic, brought the completed works of William Shakespeare and used it as the bard originally intended—as a seat cushion to make me her height.

She begged me, "Please, for the love of God, do not sit on the book."

But I couldn't hear her from seven inches down, so I took my rightful place perched atop the tome.

From there we had a textbook teenage romance: she repeatedly called me gay and her father told her not to date that "Lilliputian" or, in layman's terms, to pick on someone her own size; in exchange, I told her that her eyes were too close together and reminded her that I used to throw rocks at her as a child.

We both did track and field in high school—she was a thrower and I a long distance runner—so we spent lots of time together on the coarse grass in the middle of the finest tracks that Allegany County, New York, had to offer. Being a long distance runner makes track and field a particularly Sisyphean ordeal; you are damned to spend eternity futilely trapped in a seemingly endless cycle of turning left. The one upside to this setup was that if you had a boo on the infield, you'd pass her over and over and over again as she lovingly bellowed, "What are you running from?!?"

I've always been pretty intense, but in high school I was *intense.* Especially about running. I would train until tears were streaming down my face as I collapsed across the finish line. I used to run a mile in four minutes and forty-eight seconds (an impressive number that I definite-ly didn't just throw in this story because you rarely get opportunities to flex your high school mile times in casual conversation as an adult). With this intensity came an exhaustion that is unmatched in my current, much more sedentary, early twenties stoner dirtbag lifestyle. The physical fa-tigue made my consciousness retreat into the deepest, darkest recesses of my preindustrial, prehistoric lizard brain, which was a welcome escape from the mental torment that is being fifteen. As such, not many thoughts bubbled to the top of my psyche.

But one frigid May morning, when I ran past Emily, wheezing as I watched the dainty feminine spittle fly out of her mouth while she screamed some romantic turn of phrase about how I was a disappointment who didn't run fast enough, a remark that I almost certainly requested in my depraved teenage self-flagellation phase, five little words popped to the front of my oxygen-deprived brain: "God, I love that girl."

I finished the race, chest heaving, knees weak, drunk off adrenaline and affection. I was in love! I pondered this love for—by teenage standards—ages and ages . . . a whole five days. I spoke to my friends, telling them all about my amorous revelation. They asked the typical questions that you ask when your friend is in love, like, "Her, really?" and, "Didn't you hate each other like . . . six months ago?"

I decided that I simply had to tell her or else I would burst. So I took her back to the coffee shop where we had our first date, purely because I was a hopeless romantic and not at all because it was the only place in my hometown that would let teenagers hang out without buying anything.

Before the date, I texted her that I had something important to tell her; that way, I wouldn't be able to back out. Heart pounding, I reached across the table for her hands. I had never told a girl that I loved her before, or at least not in any context that I considered serious and genuine. I, as a tenth-grader, was much wiser and more knowledgeable about the intricacies of love than I had been as a naive and frankly foolish seventh-grader. I took a deep breath. "There's been something I've been meaning to tell you. When I ran past you the other day I thought to myself, 'I love that girl.' And I do. I love you."

This was followed by an overly pregnant pause—like, fifth trimester. I am not exaggerating when I say that neither of us spoke for a good forty-five seconds. If you tried to cut the tension with a knife, the knife would shatter. I would have been able to hear a pin drop if it weren't for the blood roaring in my ears. And then, finally, she opened her mouth, and the words I'd been dreaming of nonstop for the past five days tumbled out: "So . . . nice weather we've been having!"

If you found yourself on an alien planet and had to explain what first love feels like, how would you describe it?

"The sound of a kiss is not so loud as that of a cannon, but its echo lasts a great deal longer."

OLIVER WENDELL HOLMES

FIRST KISSES

Kassie Rubico

The kissing started the summer I turned ten. My older brother decided that David Paquin and I should be a "couple." At merely a decade, I had no idea what that meant but trusted David did—he was twelve. The first time we kissed was on the path behind my house, a hard, not quite closed-mouth kiss. What I remember most was David's oversized incisors rubbing against my equally oversized incisors. Neither of us knew what to do next, so we continued down the path to Plunkett's Drug Store to buy penny candy. We tried kissing again on the way back to my house, and again, we were all teeth.

David and I continued kissing that summer. We'd head for the path with such anticipation, which then led to awkwardness—turn my head this way or that?—and then eventually guilt. Even though my older brother didn't see our behavior as bad, something inside me said what we were doing was not right. Besides, the kissing wasn't nearly as fun as the other stuff that David and I did that summer: making forts in the back of my father's pickup truck; playing ping pong on top of the picnic table; climbing trees. David was different from other boys I knew, including my older brothers. Unlike them, David was shy, soft-spoken. His warm blue eyes sparkled whenever we'd discover some insect slinking underneath a rock.

Sometime during the fall after the summer of our first kiss, David's family moved to a new neighborhood. One night, Mom and I visited. While the adults congregated in the kitchen, David and I explored the swamp behind his new house. We sat in the tall grass just at the edge of the marsh and counted fireflies. I had never seen a firefly, and although I found them intriguing, I was much more interested in something I had overheard the grownups whispering about, something about David's father still living at the old house and something else about "a girlfriend." It didn't make sense. I wanted to ask David why a married man would have a girlfriend. But instead, I focused on his explanation of how the firefly's light was a warning signal against predators. That night in the darkness, we watched the sparks—light, then dark, then light again—neither of us at all concerned about kissing.

We kissed one more time five years after our first kiss. David and I hadn't seen each other much after the night at the swamp. I volunteered to go with Mom to visit Mrs. Paquin one night, secretly hoping that David would be there. After an awkward reunion, David suggested we go down to the basement to play pool while our moms talked in the kitchen. Downstairs, David shot balls. I was the shy one this time, self-conscious of the fact that unlike most of my friends, I had yet to run the proverbial sex bases. Standing at the edge of the pool table, I drew circles with my index finger on the green felt. David told me about his new job and how he was saving up for a used car. I talked about my track meet. He shot a ball into the corner pocket, and I blocked it from going in. We both laughed. After a while, he suggested we go outside.

In the dark shadow behind his house, I could barely see David, but I felt him when he leaned against me. When he put his hands on my waist, I felt something else, something different from that summer on the path, something other than awkwardness and shame. And when David kissed me, it was lips and tongue and no teeth at all.

I was babysitting my nephew when I got the news that David Paquin was killed in a car accident. It was a year after the kiss behind his house, the last time I had seen David. He had just started his senior year, and that night, he was on a first date with a sophomore from his school. I was told that David's car was hit head-on by a truck, that the truck's driver had fallen asleep, that the girl David was with had survived, and that David was killed instantly. My mother told me that David must have seen the truck crossing over into his lane because before it hit, he leaned in front of the girl and saved her life. Over time, I have imagined this: a girl that I did not know sitting close to David on the bench seat of his Chevy Impala. I picture David's right arm resting on the girl's shoulders. Maybe they were listening to The Moody Blues, his favorite band. I see David turning to look at the girl, his half smile, taking his eyes off the road for a split second, maybe to kiss her, and then I see him throwing his body in front of her. I have imagined myself in that car. I think about David Paquin and what might have happened had we lived in the same town, gone to the same school. Would we have been driving on those dark roads that night? If so, would it have been my life that he saved? I see myself on the seat next to David, headlights, like fireflies: there and then gone.

Write about your first kiss. Was it magical, awkward, or gross?

FIRST DANCE

Mitch Applebaum

Many years ago, my good friend Joe introduced me to contra dancing. "Huh," I said. "What's that?" And I thought, *Shit, I can't dance.* But I knew Joe, a very average-looking guy, had done pretty well with the women at these dances.

Turns out, contra dancing is an easier combination of square and swing dancing. If you can walk and follow directions at the same time, you can contra dance—sort of like Dancing For Dummies. There is always a caller and live band. You dance for forty seconds in groups of four—you, your partner, and the neighboring couple. When you finish, you face a new couple and do the same steps with them, and so on. Each dance lasts about ten minutes and then you change partners.

While contra dancing is not a singles' event, many people go alone because the get-togethers are a good way to meet people of the opposite sex (if you get my drift :-)). The weekly dance takes place in The Church of the Village downtown. The atmosphere is relaxed and inviting, which in New York City is like finding a cop when you need one.

So I started going and I *was* meeting people, but not "quite" the right one. Are you following me here? I'd been contra dancing for three years when things finally changed. One night, I was at a dance and I thought there was no one I was interested in meeting, but I figured that was okay as it was still three hours of fun and I was having a good time.

Towards the end of the evening I finished a dance, properly thanked my partner, and turned around to look for my next partner. Standing before me was a smiling, attractive, age-appropriate lady with pretty hazel eyes and brunette bangs (I am a sucker for bangs) whom I hadn't noticed before. I asked her to dance and she said yes. Because we paired up immediately, we had a few minutes to talk. I learned her name was Judy and she was a native New Yorker currently living in Kentucky and visiting her family here. Judy had gotten to the dance very late, which is why I hadn't noticed her earlier. I also learned she had a master's degree in piano performance, spoke three languages, and that there are three different ways to pronounce Louisville. I already liked her.

So the dance started. I'll just say it—I felt a connection. We shared good eye contact and lots of smiles. She even laughed at my bad jokes. When the dance ended, we thanked each other, and I was pretty sure she felt the pull too.

As an aside, we danced the *penultimate* dance of the evening. (Just so you know, *penultimate* is my favorite word. It means the second to the last in a series of things.) Judy and I each danced the last dance with different partners. And then the night was over.

I made sure to tell Judy that a bunch of dancers always went to the Village Diner afterwards and I asked her if she wanted to go. She agreed. We gathered our things and as we walked up the church steps and out of the basement, we fell immediately into a nice, natural conversation. Things were looking good. Maybe all this contra dancing was going to pay off. We got about three steps onto the sidewalk when the night took a turn.

As if he fell from the sky, another male dancer was now walking on the other side of Judy. I was thinking, *What the fuck*? Didn't this guy know the man code? Didn't he know he needed to wait for me to strike out before he hit on Judy? And I was actually doing pretty well with the beautiful brunette. I was ahead in the count.

This guy was wearing a bright red flannel shirt over his barrel chest and had a ZZ Top wannabe beard. I didn't know what to do. Should I have said something? On the one hand he was intruding on our conversation; on the other hand, the sidewalks were public domain. What was Judy thinking? Would she say something? Maybe she preferred guys in bright red flannel shirts with ZZ Top wannabe beards. I didn't know what Judy liked. As it turned out, neither one of us said anything.

In the four-minute walk to the diner, this guy had very little to say, but we did learn his name was Paul. The diner always has a big table set up for us in the back so all the dancers can sit together. On the way to the table, I noticed an empty booth. I asked Judy if she'd like to sit there. She said yes. The booth was going to accomplish two things: One, it was going to give Judy and me some privacy, and two, it was going to allow Paul a chance to make a graceful exit and make him understand that he took his shot and it just wasn't happening for him. So I waved Judy onto the bench and she slid down. I sat on the opposite bench so that I was directly in front of her. Lo and behold, I looked to my right and there was Paul sitting next to Judy. The clue phone was ringing but Paul was not picking up.

Again Paul had very little to say, but Judy and I were having a wonderful get-to-know you conversation in spite of Paul's presence. After about an hour, we all paid our respective checks and left the diner. I was hoping Paul would finally bug off, but as you probably already suspect, he didn't. Three we were again—The Three Musketeers—walking down Seventh Avenue.

Now I started to panic. It was midnight, and I wanted to ask Judy out, but not in front of Paul. Hey, I know rejection. Rejection and I have become friends. We sometimes have dinner together. But public rejection was not exactly on my bucket list. My only hope, since we were about three blocks from the subway, was that Paul would disappear into the bowels of Manhattan, and I could ask Judy out privately.

But that didn't happen. However, I did catch a small break, because the traffic light turned red just as we reached the corner, which bought me a little time. The three of us stood there awkwardly. I was tense, but I said to myself, "Screw it." I wasn't going to let Paul ruin my chance at a date with Judy.

So . . . drumroll here . . . I asked her out in front of Paul. Before Judy could answer, Paul said, and I quote, "I won't ask you out. I'll just say goodnight," and into the subway he went like he was racing off to the ZZ Top concert.

How's that for an unusual first meeting? I'll say three things to wrap it up: one—Judy said yes; two—eighteen months later we got married; and three—we decided not to invite Paul to the wedding because we were afraid he would try to sit at the head table and cut in on the first dance!

YOU NEVER KNOW WHERE YOU'LL FIND LOVE.

Locate the differences in the two pictures.

MY FIRST HUSBAND

Holly Rutchik

"❝I don't want my wife managing me," my first husband said to his therapist. I had accepted the invitation to one of his therapy sessions, but now that I was there, it felt like being called to the principal's office.

"Would you agree some people need managing?" his therapist asked with a raised eyebrow as she sipped her coffee.

Those words had escaped my own lips just that morning. My credit card had recently been declined at a furniture store as I balanced four toddlers and a giant mattress atop a shopping cart. I'd finally convinced him to get tested for adult ADHD.

"I don't want her to have to manage me," he shot back at her. His giant blue eyes bore into me, but the bullet of his words was aimed at the therapist. To him, his ability to love me was being questioned.

To me, she was stating the obvious. He needed me, and I needed him. That's love. Why was he so upset?

As an absent-minded professor with a creative soul and a genius brain, loving me came naturally to my first husband. He was too frugal to order a soda in a restaurant because "it's sugar water marked up six hundred percent," but he always ordered me Diet Coke. He'd save $3.50 there but accrue a monthly late fee on a forgotten bill.

On paper, we had less than our middle-class counterparts. We were less healthy, less social, less financially stable, and less organized.

We had the most, though. Everyone who spent time with us knew it. Our life was hard, but we had an epic type of love. We were the couple others envied. Friends sought us out for marriage advice. Best friends turned lovers, we shared similar interests, passions, and faith. We could be alone together in silence or talk all night. The "no one has ever been this in love" feeling that eventually wears off for couples when life gets hard or things start to sag never wore off for us.

"I'm sorry I can't give you everything," he'd say, apologizing for not being a trust fund baby. I'd laugh and remind him he wasn't a knight, nor was I a princess. We weren't fairy tale material. We could never hoist ourselves onto a horse's saddle. If, by some miracle, we did manage, we'd break the poor horse's back with our bellies and our baggage.

We gave each other everything we had—more than we should have. We were inebriated in love.

"Don't worry," I'd joke when he wished for a life void of responsibilities for me. "My next husband will take care of that. You're only my first husband—the one to have kids with, so they'll be kind and brilliant."

Neither one of us could have been with anyone else. We saw each other's faults and loved the other in their mess. "I love you, madly," he'd say. "Madly," I'd repeat.

I managed his calendar. He managed the kids' early mornings and all my moods.

He believed his call was to help me achieve my dreams—that they were bigger than his own.

He never answered his phone. It was always lost. We were often late because he SWORE he put his keys on the counter and was genuinely surprised when they were found in the bathroom. When it was no longer sustainable for me to stay home with our kids, I got myself a job writing and started climbing every ladder I could find.

He trusted me wholeheartedly, even when I was wrong. With my vision and his willpower, we found ways to make the impossible possible. He called me his black magic woman. He held down the fort when I burned out and let me take to our bed and wallow like a pale, chubby Victorian woman who had fallen ill.

Once, we forgot to deposit my paycheck and then misplaced it. It was intended for our monthly groceries and diapers. Our most feral child found it and used it as a teething toy, leaving it in gummed-up clumps on the floor. We were without food until a new check arrived.

Hungry bellies underfoot, I blamed my first husband for all the things that were both our fault. While I carried on, he invented something to call dinner. I cried while he browned freezer-burned turkey meat and threw in what little food we had: canned diced tomatoes, frozen hash browns, and corn. Half a bag of questionable cheese. He presented "everything skillet" like it was a Michelin star restaurant meal. It looked like prison food. We went to bed full and laughing.

My first husband was the magic one. He shouldered difficult things silently. I was a bit more vocal about life's misfortunes—and my perseverance over them.

Both wordsmiths, when we fought, we did it well.

"Crap falls out of our van and our house when we open the doors," I yelled at him once.

"You care too much about what people think," he said.

"Well, you care too little," I replied. "I'm not carrying designer purses! We shop at Big Lots and we have a literal litter of children!"

He didn't care what other people thought. Just me. He taught me that's how I deserve to be loved.

Last year, at forty, my first husband left us with our house still full of young kids.

"I'm so sorry I'm leaving you," he said.

"You're not cleaning out our bank account, going out for milk, and skipping town." I laughed. "You're dying."

Even on his deathbed, I was his priority. He asked when I'd last eaten and when I'd last read. He knew how important my nighttime book routine was to my mental health. He also understood how stressed I got about water getting into our basement and potentially ruining my tomes. So when a new bookshelf was delivered for our lower level, he summoned all his breath and energy to ensure the shelves were placed on risers. He wouldn't be here to help the next time the basement flooded.

I think of my first husband every time I lose my phone, which is now daily. "It's Daddy!" the kids joke.

"He's pranking you!"

"It IS Daddy!" I growl.

He may be dead, but things can still be all his fault. I still love him madly and make the "everything skillet" weekly. My first husband absolutely ruined me. It's why he'll likely be my only. I'm so annoyed with him about it.

*"There is always
some madness in love.
But there is also
some reason in madness."*

FRIEDRICH NIETZSCHE

MODEL BEHAVIOR

Robin Eileen Bernstein

Many years ago when I was nineteen, I moved off campus for my third year of college in upstate New York. My next-door neighbor was a student too, so I saw him around a lot.

Craig was tall, almost gawky, as if he'd just grown into his adult body and wasn't quite used to it. He seemed nice enough at first, and very chatty, until it hit me that he only seemed to chat about himself. And tell jokes that weren't funny, at least to me. So, I kept this new neighbor with the big ego at a neighborly distance.

After a month of next-door-neighbor chitchat, he asked me out. I said I was busy. When he asked me out again a week or two later, I said yes. I figured, okay, I'd give him a chance. Or maybe he just wore me down.

The date was a Saturday in late October, dinner at his place. I walked the thirty seconds from my house to his, where he'd set a lovely table and prepared a nice meal. But to my disappointment, he once again droned on and on about his life, until I wanted to catapult myself home.

After dinner, I helped with the dishes and said I had to leave, blaming my abrupt departure on an upcoming exam. I studied a lot back then. There was no making out. No kissing. No nothing. The next day I summed up the date in my green diary: "Not interested."

One reason I studied a lot was because I was frustrated. I was a drummer, but without a band. I yearned for a semester abroad, but never applied. And my love life was going nowhere, fast. I did, however, manage to find a truly awful part-time job working the night shift at McDonald's. My blue polyester uniform reeked of french fry grease no matter how often I washed it. I'd take the bus home at 11:00 p.m., my head pressed against the window, wondering why I couldn't get my act together.

The only thing I loved that year was my figure drawing class. Rendering nudes in charcoal was as close to Zen as I got. Craig asked me out once or twice more and I politely declined, hoping he'd get the hint. The morning after Valentine's Day, which I no doubt spent studying, I missed the bus to campus. Running late to my drawing class, I stood at the end of my block hitching, as we students often did; other students almost always picked us up. My neighbor, who had a car, saw me with my thumb out. He rolled down his window and offered me a ride. I accepted.

The drive was maybe five minutes. We chatted pleasantly. Or rather he chatted pleasantly—about himself, of course. When we got to campus, he swerved into the first parking spot he saw and jumped out.

"Gotta run or I'll be late," he said, sprinting away like a VIP. I barely had time to say thanks.

"I'm late, too," I called out, but he was too far away to hear me.

By the time I got to my drawing class, the model was already on the platform, bare buttocks facing me. Embarrassed by my tardiness, I kept my head down and made a beeline for the one remaining spot at the far end of the room. The only sound was charcoal scratching on paper. I placed my pad on my easel and looked up.

My jaw dropped.

The model was Craig. He was staring at me. And I was staring at . . . everything I'd been missing.

If the ground had opened and swallowed me whole, I would have been grateful. I'm guessing he felt likewise.

Yet I managed to make this already awkward situation even worse. I drew him—head, torso, limbs, hands, feet—but deliberately, and quite obviously, omitted a certain male part of his anatomy. Cut his ego down to size, ha ha, I giggled to myself.

During the break, he put on a robe and walked around the room, glancing at each student's work. Eventually he got to me.

"Nice," he said.

Was that sarcasm? My normally chatty neighbor said nothing more. An icy shame rose in my belly—the painful realization that there was nothing humorous about what I'd just done.

He had offered us his body, and this was how I thanked him? For all I knew, he was as frustrated with his life as I was with mine. Maybe he babbled on about himself because he was anxious or insecure. Meanwhile, like a jerk, I'd made this about me and my wants, wounding someone whose only crime was liking me. Who was the unfunny, self-centered one now?

I wanted to apologize but the words stuck in my throat.

Drawing requires that you learn to see. Really see. And on that chilly February morning, I saw much more than my neighbor's nude body. I finally was able to see a fellow student struggling, as I was, to make his way in this messy world. We were both exposed that day, two flawed and vulnerable young people—a man and woman about to leave adolescence behind—each of us stumbling along a well-traveled road toward adulthood, searching for connection and fulfillment. And maybe even someone to love.

MAKE THIS HEART WHOLE.

Draw the other half.

SHIFTY DAN

Ivy Eisenberg

I come home to my grad school apartment one afternoon, and there on my sofa is a shifty-eyed, wiry guy with creepy blue-tinted glasses and one of those seventies haircuts, with the recalcitrant frizzy hair that sticks out on either side like tufts of steel wool. He's wearing tan cutoffs—I mean he actually cut his trousers to make shorts—and he's sitting on my white couch with no underwear and his sweaty balls peeking out and looking at me like I'm the intruder.

"I'm Dan," he announces. "I'm Bart's friend."

Bart is one of my roommates. I'm twenty-four years old, a student at Penn State in State College, Pennsylvania, a town known as Happy Valley—where I am chronically not happy. I have no friends, I'm lost in life, I hate football, and I'm sharing an apartment with weirdos: a townie waitress, her drug-dealing boyfriend, and Burnout Bart, an undergrad.

Bart asks if Dan can crash on our couch for a few days—since I'm the one who brought that couch into the place. At this moment, I have written off the couch for good. Eww. Whatever. I am swamped with work and school. I don't care what Dan does.

For the next couple of days, every time I walk through our apartment, there's Shifty Dan, hanging out, with his tan underwear-less cutoffs,

27

watching me with his beady eyes. When I leave for work, he's there. When I get home? There he is. I can feel him forming opinions about me. You know those judgy types. Doesn't he have anywhere to go?

It comes out that Dan has just gotten out of jail, after spending seven years in prison for armed robbery of convenience stores. My couch is his first stop in the free world. Oh, he's an honest guy, says Bart—would never rip off a friend. No worries about my belongings. No, it's the establishment, evil corporations that he's against.

Shifty Dan is quite the know-it-all. He's an expert about politics, history, economics.

And Dan fashions himself as a great Scrabble player. Wait a minute. Scrabble is *my* game. Somehow, Dan thinks that his seven years in the state penitentiary has made him a better Scrabble player than my seven years as an English major. Oh, bitch, the challenge is on.

First game, there we are under the fluorescent lights of the dining room, at the square folding table, which is our dining table. Dan pulls a seven-letter word with a *Z*—rhizome—finding a loose word to place the *E* under and getting that word too. Impressive, yes, but I manage to eke out a seven-letter word on triple word score—and grab a vertical play at the *Z* with the word *fez*. Fez—yeah, it is a word, sir. I've won.

The next night, there we are again. Shifty Dan wins. Twice.

I'm furious. I stew about it all the next day, thinking about words constantly, thumbing through the dictionary in my office, looking at the awnings downtown—obsessively moving things around on the imaginary wooden rack in my brain. Here's a seven-letter word—*ASSHOLE*.

Our nightly Scrabble dates go on for a couple of weeks. I find myself looking forward to them, canceling other plans, and—dare I say, sort of dressing up a bit for the game. Gauzy, see-through tops—that sort of thing.

One night, about a month into this, I propose to Dan that we play for stakes. Best of three. And the loser will be a servant for a day for the winner. Am I flirting with this guy? Have I lost my mind? I win the first game.

He wins the second game. The third game? He wins. He is the master, and I am the servant. I cannot imagine what will happen, but I am prepared for the worst, and by that I mean I shave my armpits.

Servant day is innocent. Somehow, though, within a few days, we start hooking up—Dan's best score yet. Shifty Dan is now living in my bedroom. We move to a cheap summer sublet with bare necessities: a few utensils, pans, the Scrabble set, dictionary, all my stuff, and Dan's cutoff shorts. We have fun hanging out and having weird, creepy, Shifty Dan sex—very pleasant, but with some rules, like no tongue. Weird.

I take Dan to meet my nice Jewish parents in suburban Long Island. It is obvious that Dan is not Jewish, neither a doctor, a lawyer, or employed—anywhere.

My parents' panic-stricken looks are a shock to my system. A light-bulb goes off and I see another seven-letter word: *FREEDOM*. I'm almost twenty-five years old. I have shit to do. Even if it means that I will be alone again, I have to dump this guy. So I quit Shifty Dan and take a leave of absence from school.

Dan winds up in the slammer again. I'm spooked, sad, and relieved, and against all odds, and to the surprise of the English department, I return to complete my degree.

I become a woman of letters—and not just letter tiles. Oh, I'm still a kick-ass Scrabble player! Those letters become words, become sentences, paragraphs and the stories of my life.

Write about a time you did something, or were involved with someone, in the "name of love" that didn't feel in alignment with your true nature. What did you learn from the experience?

"Fate leads him who follows it,
and drags him who resists."

PLUTARCH

COMET IS CUPID

Stacy Alderman

"It's me or the dog," Jennifer said. Unbeknownst to me, a guy named Jay was trying to salvage an unhealthy relationship with his long-time, live-in girlfriend named Jennifer. It was a union that had been on the rocks for years.

Jay had wanted a dog for months, so he decided to surprise Jennifer by adopting a shelter pup. As Jay walked among the cages, peering at the forlorn animals, he returned again and again to a blond and white mutt who was nothing short of pathetic. The dog barely raised its head when he passed by, but the dejected look in its brown eyes tugged at Jay's heartstrings.

"What's up, buddy?" Jay whispered, crouching in front of its cage.

The sad dog peered into Jay's soul and let out a pitiful whimper.

An hour later, the mutt had a new owner and a new name—Comet, after one of the reindeer in the holiday song that was on the radio on the drive home. Jay couldn't wait to introduce the pup to Jennifer.

She hated Comet from the get-go. Hated that Jay had picked him without her. Hated that the canine chewed on books and pillows. Hated that he didn't listen to her. She accused Comet of growling at her after she smacked him on his vaccine-sore butt.

That snarl was the last straw for Jennifer.

"It's me or the dog!" she threatened over the phone as Jay drove to work.

Jay stewed about Jennifer's ultimatum all day. Comet was the sweetest dog he'd ever met. An animal lover his entire life, Jay had made a vow that he would never abandon a pet.

He reviewed all that had been wrong in his relationship with Jennifer. He thought about the many attempts he'd made to fix things, and the nights he'd ended up at his parents' house after big fights.

But with Jennifer's demand, something changed. After a lot of soul-searching, Jay knew that surrendering Comet would be more painful than ending the unhealthy romantic relationship.

Jay packed up all of his belongings, and with Comet in tow, moved in with his mom and dad. The breakup was hard and Jay was lonely, but Comet's companionship made the transition easier.

After a few months, Jay's coworkers, Chris and his girlfriend Kelley, noticed a positive change in Jay, so Kelley asked if Jay was ready to start dating again. She suspected that this sweet, hilarious guy would be perfect for someone she'd known for a long time.

That someone was me.

"I think you should meet our coworker," Kelley suggested. "He's really funny and loves hockey."

I had sworn off dating—for good. At twenty-three years old, I had just been blown off by another jerk. And I was done.

"He needs someone like you," Kelley insisted. "He recently got out of a bad relationship."

Great, I thought. Guys fresh out of difficult relationships were exactly the kind of men I didn't want to meet.

Reluctantly, I agreed to a double-dinner date at Chris' apartment. That night, I wore my most boring pair of jeans and barely put on any makeup. After years of primping before every outing, I'd given up trying to look perfect for undeserving guys who would probably let me down.

My expectations for the evening could not have been lower. Surprisingly, the conversation flowed, and we shared lots of laughs. Once we'd finished eating, we headed to a local dive bar.

There was something different about Jay—his kind eyes, his engaging smile, and his quick wit. But it was the unabashed affection in his voice when he talked about Comet that I found most charming.

When Kelley and I escaped to the bar's bathroom together, I couldn't hide my grin. I didn't want to get my hopes up, but I had to admit that I was having fun and I didn't want the evening to end.

Matchmaker Kelley asked Jay to drive me home. Our effortless banter filled the car and my heart fluttered. When he pulled into my driveway, I didn't hesitate. I leaned over and kissed him.

"So I guess it's okay for me to ask for your number?" he asked, his voice bordering on shy for the first time all night.

I laughed as he punched my number into his Samsung slider phone.

I'll never forget the thrill that blazed through me when he called the next day . . . and the day after that. It wasn't long before I met his parents—and Comet.

The first time I tried to sit next to Jay on the couch, Comet plopped down between us and almost pushed me onto the floor, protecting his dad.

It only took a few more visits and belly rubs for me to win Comet's approval. The first time I said, "Lie down," and he obeyed, snuggling into my lap, my heart melted.

The rest, as they say, is history.

Jay and I have been married for eleven years. After thirteen happy years with Jay and then me, Comet crossed the rainbow bridge in his own bed surrounded by his humans.

While I will be forever indebted to Kelley and Chris for setting up the blind date that brought Jay and me together, I can't deny I am grateful that Comet and Jennifer didn't get along. That dog was Cupid and he shot an arrow through Jay's heart that landed squarely into mine. And for that we are endlessly grateful.

BLIND DATE

Sarah Squires-Doyle

"At the very least, we should meet for a lunch date just to appease Nishi. After all, it's not like we're getting married," Mike's first email read.

It was cold that December and I was bracing myself for yet another dreaded holiday season. Single again and almost forty years old, my hopes for finding love, marriage, and starting a family were becoming a distant fantasy.

Frozen, I looked at the computer screen and reread Mike's email. My fingers shook, my heart thundered and I typed, "yes."

My marriage clock had been ticking. Each swing of the pendulum louder and louder. Doom felt near. A few weeks ago, I'd made a deal with the universe. I ran to my favorite spot on the lakefront. With my arms flailing and tears streaming down my cheeks, I'd pleaded to the powers that be, "I will stop dating the *bad boys,* the ones who treat me like crap. Please send a *nice guy*. I promise I'll give him a chance."

And then, shortly after my waterside meltdown, a long-time friend, Nishi, insisted on setting me up on a blind date with his high school buddy Mike. Nishi was certain we had enough in common to be a good match—similar in age, we were good people who loved running and volunteering for the Chicago Marathon. I agreed, half-heartedly.

I found out later that Nishi (after too many beers one night) had thumbed through his cerebral-let's-find-Mike-a-date rolodex and pulled my proverbial card. Nevertheless, I appreciated Mike's sense of humor and found myself laughing out loud as I read his wittily-crafted paragraphs. His personality and honesty jumped through the screen.

Our first "meeting" was at The Chicago Diner, a well-known meat-free establishment since 1983, and one I'd never stepped foot in. Did I really agree to go on a blind date? With a vegan? Skepticism reared its ugly head again.

I arrived at the restaurant with jitters in my stomach. The smiling host walked me back to meet my date in a cozy red booth. Leaping up to greet me, Mike seemed genuinely excited and fired so many questions that I wasn't sure if we were on a date or an interview. But his curiosity was refreshing. It felt sincere, respectful, and . . . different! Admittedly, I occasionally thought, who is this alien? Was I in the presence of the ever-elusive, rarely-spotted nice guy?

And when I glanced at my watch and realized we had been talking for over three hours, I didn't care that my parking meter had long expired. He asked if we could meet again and I said yes, then we walked to my car as a smile washed over my blushing face.

Then we began a series of day dates that would start with lunch and continue well beyond dinner. We loved frolicking through our big city, taking in museums, restaurants, and Millenium Park.

A year later, in front of our 180 wedding guests, Mike sang (Elvis twang and all), "Love Me Tender" as my heart melted. We had written our own vows, but conceded that we were allowed to improvise. Turns out our Second City comedy training came in handy. Mike, a master at impersonations, broke into occasional caveman grunts and Rocky Balboa slurs as we delivered our lines, which curbed my running emotions and got us to the finish line. We co-produced what felt like a variety show rather than a commitment ceremony, but we had the time of our lives. We danced the night away and soon had a baby girl on the way.

When you open your heart and your mind, you often discover what you are looking for. It's never too late to find love or ask the universe for a little help. And a *nice guy.*

Have you ever gone on a blind date? If so, write about what it was like the moment you saw your mystery partner. If not, would you go on a blind date? Why or why not?

WHEN LOOKING FOR LOVE . . .

Find these qualities!

```
E N T H U S I A S M E T
C X E F N H O P E K A E
O M S R G A V F I A K N
M J M I E N I L N S I D
M R I E D S C A I I N E
U E L N W E P R E S D R
N D E D A D S E T T N N
I N S S R F H I C O E E
C O A H M R U G R T S S
A W R I T E M N E E S S
T F I P H C O O V E X U
I I N T E G R I T Y E A
O S A F E T Y W A N T W
N H U G S K I S S E S E
```

TENDERNESS SMILES ENTHUSIASM LIKE HOPE
RESPECT DESIRE RISK HUMOR FUN FRIENDSHIP
KINDNESS AWE SAFETY INTEGRITY WANT
COMMUNICATION WARMTH HUGS KISSES WONDER

"To love yourself is the beginning
of a lifelong romance."

OSCAR WILDE

WHO WE THOUGHT WE'D BE

Cara Alwill

My mother loves to tell a story about me. I'm around four years old, sitting in my grandparents' kitchen decked out in my grandmother's red feather boa, blonde wig, and giant sunglasses. I order my grandfather to "interview" me as I sit on a bar stool and tell him my name is Dagmar (my grandmother's name) and I am an actress from Hollywood. "I have no children," I say, and glare at my mother in disgust.

I can remember, as far back as around junior high school, thinking that I would be a divorcée when I grew up. Not because I thought I'd fail at marriage, but because I truly idolized divorced women. In my mind, divorcées were rich and glamorous and independent. They drank wine and smoked cigarettes and wore fur coats and had affairs with hot younger men who worshiped them. They didn't have the time or interest in being a wife. They definitely had long red nails that clicked and clacked and their fingers were dressed in shiny jewels.

I'm sure I created this fantasy after watching daytime soap operas after school in my grandparents' kitchen while Dagmar, a platinum blonde bombshell always dressed to the nines and dripping in gold, served us Entenmann's pound cake and Lipton tea with cream and sugar.

Dagmar herself was a divorcée, at that point on her second marriage with my grandfather, while simultaneously having an affair with her ex-husband, Tony. I didn't know the intricacies of her romantic life at the time, but there was an energy radiating from her that screamed: *Men are disposable and certainly not the most important thing.*

My mother became a divorcée when I was eight years old. I'd sneak into the hallway of our apartment and listen to her phone conversations while she chain-smoked Newport Lights by the kitchen window. "Cocksucker," she'd say, describing my father or some other man. *Cocksucker.* I had never heard that word before, but I loved it.

Divorcées had something that I found so alluring—power. They were desired, so much so that someone wanted to *marry* them and be with them forever. Yet they rejected the notion when it stopped working for them. In a world where little girls are groomed to be brides and being single is often looked upon as a disease, divorcées completely flipped the script.

But to become a divorcée, I'd have to get married first. I met my ex-husband in December of 2009 on a dating website called OkCupid, and on Valentine's Day in 2011, we were standing on top of the Empire State Building, exchanging vows in an elaborate ceremony we won after I wrote and submitted an essay about our "Iconic Love" to The Knot.com. *Our love is as timeless as the Empire State Building*, I wrote, and I believed it.

Ryan and I fell in love fast. Our first kiss was on New Year's Eve at a dive bar in the East Village. He moved in with me two months later, and the first half of our marriage was exciting and filled with passion. We were obsessed with each other, and spent many nights drinking wine and laughing and having sex.

He helped me build my business and I helped him reinvent himself after a successful freestyle motocross career that came to an end due to his physical injuries. We were a team. But we were also both changing, fast.

He was adapting to a desk job, finding it harder and harder to feel that spark that he once had from flipping over dirtbikes in Los Angeles.

My spark had turned into a fire, once my blog took off and I began publishing my books.

We began to grow apart, like so many couples do. We tried, unsuccessfully, to keep our marriage alive for years beyond its expiration date. Eventually, the version of our Iconic Love that was essential to a marriage ran its course and by 2020, I had reached my goal. I was finally a divorcée.

I'm now forty-three, divorced, have no children (by choice), glamorous when I want to exchange my yoga pants for a silk dress or something like that, not exactly rich but definitely okay, and a writer. I live in Manhattan with three doormen and a fancy stove that I still don't know how to work.

I've had hot, young *lovers* (I fucking love that word) and literally just went to Hollywood a few months ago to be interviewed on a panel about my career.

But even though I've become the divorcée I've always wanted to be, I don't believe men are disposable and unimportant. In fact, getting divorced has made me fall more in love with love than ever before.

Getting my divorce was the biggest act of love—for both me and my ex. We weren't happy anymore, and we both deserved a chance to find real, true love again. We both deserved the chance to come back to ourselves.

It's been four years. I haven't found the romantic love I long for just yet, but I know I'm close. I'm still kind of fumbling through it all. I'm making mistakes and choosing the wrong people from time to time. I'm getting my heart broken and I'm breaking hearts and it can be messy. But it is always, always worth it.

I've met a new version of myself and she's not the callous, man-hating ice queen I always envisioned she'd be. But she is still powerful. Powerful enough to trust herself. Powerful enough to walk away from what's not working. Powerful enough to love herself first. Powerful enough to never, ever settle for anything less than everything she wants.

EVERLY-AFTER

Raven Petretti-Stamper

I saw Darrin, my ex-boyfriend, in line at Whole Foods. I couldn't believe it. I pinched my cheeks, pushed up my boobs, and called his name, and when he turned around I said, "Look at us. The dynamic duo together again."

He asked if we could go outside to catch up and told me I looked fantastic. I did. I had drowned my sorrows at the gym after we broke up years ago, so I thanked him and apologized for needing to stretch after my jog. (Any excuse to throw my toned ass in his face.) He started pooh-poohing about how he had let himself go. It was true—he looked like the statue of David but with a beer gut.

We talked. I felt so bad and kept thinking his life took a total nosedive since we broke up. I said something to that extent and he said, "Oh, you mean when we did hard time?"

I couldn't believe he was likening our love to being in prison. He immediately apologized and said he needed to go and I was like, "Wait, I haven't told you anything about me. Like I bought a place on Central Park West and yes, you should be simmering in jealousy. It's spectacular. Muuuuuuch better than your messy place."

He said his place looked better now that he got a roommate.

"Who is it? Why would a perennial bachelor like you decide to get a roommate?" And he again tried to say goodbye and walk away, so I said, "Please. I'd love to hear more about your roommate . . . "

He was now visibly uncomfortable and stuttering but he told me he liked *him*—a lot. The guy was such a commitment phobe of course his roommate was a guy. He told me *he* cleans and cooks and what's not to love about that and we left the subject behind. We moved on to the night when we'd made pesto ravioli. I asked if he remembered what he had said then. It was forever ago . . . but that was a big night for us. He had said he wanted to be with me forever.

"We had such a good thing." I smiled.

"We really did," Darrin agreed.

I wasn't sure how we wound up like we did, so I needed to hear that from him.

And then he put his left hand on my arm to comfort me and I saw his wedding ring.

I tried to collect myself. "Pull it together," I said in my head. "Don't be mad. You are not to yell at him with your eyes." But I was so angry, and I struck out as if our split had been yesterday.

"I get that you were trying not to hurt my feelings but that roommate-is-a-roommate thing was too much. Forget that it didn't work out for us because you got cold feet about getting married. Please be careful what you say next. Please don't tell me you finally met the right person."

I stared at him, my heart breaking all over again. "Who on earth did you marry? I said if you want to get married, propose already because I thought you would propose *to me*. I didn't mean to inspire you to marry someone else. Christ, next thing you're gonna do is tell me you have children."

And he did. His wife gave birth to their youngest a month ago. The wife he tried to pass off as a male roommate earlier.

"You really did the whole thing," I muttered. "Well, my life's not all doom and gloom. I own a business and—the apartment. Right. I told you about the apartment. Both are amazing. Fulfilling. Wonderful. Everything I ever dreamed of. Work is exactly what I need. I'm too busy for people and their bullshit."

I wanted so badly to ask if he was nervous on his big day. If he thought I'd walk through the door because I'm always so dramatic.

Instead I said, "Goodbye, Darrin." I tucked my broken heart back where it belonged and walked away. I didn't know it yet, but my true love was waiting for me. He just needed me to find myself first.

Write about a situation when you stayed in a relationship past its expiration date.

LOVE UNDER WRAPS

Franklin Matthews

How does a theater-loving homosexual explain a green-card gay marriage to his conservative, evangelical parents whose happy coupling exceeds the Broadway runs of *Cats* and *Phantom of the Opera* combined?

Simple: He keeps quiet.

So of course, confusion and panic struck the day I awoke from knee surgery with my mom and dad, my husband, and my boyfriend at the foot of my hospital bed. What show was this—and where was the script?

To quote *A Chorus Line*: "Let's do the whole combination from the top."

One night a few years prior, I'd been out with friends. Midtown Manhattan—more specifically, Hell's Kitchen—was my bar-hopping beat, especially. After friends and I parted ways, I strolled solo into Posh, a favorite haunt, for a nightcap. As the bartender mixed my Manhattan, I saw my future ex-husband sitting alone at the end of the bar. I approached and asked his name, which was Tim. I learned that this cute Vietnamese guy was in the US on a student visa. Tim loved to cook and had big entrepreneurial goals to open a restaurant. After more drinks, we exchanged numbers and left. In typical gay fashion, neither of us contacted the other. Days later, I was at Posh again—so was Tim. This time we planned dinner.

We went on another date. Soon, we were dating-slash-hanging-out-slash-I wasn't sure what *it* was.

"I'm moving to Los Angeles in June," I told Tim. I wanted to come clean before this went any further.

"You'll be back. You won't like it. Believe me," he declared with the conviction of television psychic Miss Cleo.

After a dewy-eyed adieu, I assured Tim we'd keep in touch and headed west, fully prepared to leave the frenzied metropolitan. Over the next few months, the romance fizzled but our friendship remained. Turns out, California was not for me and in exactly one year, I moved back to Manhattan, sheepishly admitting to the clairvoyant Asian that he was right.

New York State had just enacted gay marriage and over drinks with Tim, he told me that his visa expired. If he left the States, which he wanted to do because he hadn't seen his family in eight years, he wouldn't be allowed back into the country. He asked if I would marry him for a green card. I immediately dismissed the idea, my internal monologue screaming, "Insult the sanctity and institute of marriage? Never!" But did I have a calendar chock-full of proposals?

I said yes.

My neuroses and paranoia caused us to move in together. If the authorities came for us, I didn't want to be thrown in prison with guys who wouldn't appreciate my vocal selections from *Chicago* the musical.

Our rainy wedding, attended by a few close friends, took place at City Hall. That night we dined at a fancy joint, watched *The Amazing Spider-Man 2* on the big screen, came home, hugged, and then quickly retired to our separate beds. Romantic? Hardly. Practical? Yaaaaaaaaas. Covert to family? Definitely. I'd been out to them for years. They even met and liked Tim. While they were never fully accepting of my homosexuality, they had come a long way. But I knew that for them, the idea of me marrying a man would end like a Greek tragedy if they were to find out. Tim and I were "good friends" in their minds.

My husband and I agreed that we could see other people and thanks to Tinder, I swiped right on Ivan. We matched! We texted, talked, and met all in the same night. Ivan was a doctor, born in Taiwan and educated there and in the States. This guy was thoughtful, whip-smart, funny as hell, and possessed a smile so radiant, the highest SPF couldn't shield it.

"I have a confession to make," Ivan blurted during our initial encounter in his apartment. "My real name isn't Ivan. It's Darius. I created a fake profile name because I'm protective of my professional life."

"Makes sense," I replied. This was my window! "Ummm . . . while we're on the topic of confessions . . ."

Darius graciously understood and accepted my I've-married-my-good-friend-so-he-can-get-a-green-card situation. In the words of Cole Porter, "So in love with him was I."

Six months into our courtship, I needed orthopedic surgery, which required a three-month recovery.

"Since you have a walk-up and I live in an elevator building, it only makes sense that you recover at my place," my new sweetheart Darius offered.

"Let me get this right," Mom said. "You'll stay with your friend Darius for three months. He's going to take care of you and do laundry?"

"Correct." I guiltily smiled.

"What about Tim?" she inquired, suspicion in her eyes.

"Okay. We're not together anymore," I confessed. "Darius and I are."

"But you're still living with Tim?" Her brow furrowed.

I nodded.

"I'm so confused," she uttered with exhaustion.

But she and my father came to New York, intent on being there post-surgery. My secret boyfriend, Darius (whom they would meet for the first time), and my undercover husband, Tim, would escort them while I was under the knife. I debriefed them both on the hush-hush situation.

Skillfully, they navigated the duplicitous terrain—at least I think they did. In my groggy haze of anesthesia, there were no histrionics. Tim and I fulfilled our legal obligation, and we happily divorced. He became a doctor of Holistic Medicine and remains in the United States. We're still friends. Darius and I recently marked our seventh anniversary.

My parents just celebrated fifty-five wonderful years. If you ever meet them, take the advice from *Cabaret's* Sally Bowles: "Don't tell mama. Whatever you do."

"Every new beginning comes
from other beginnings' end."

SENECA

THIS IS NOT NORMAL

Amy Impellizzeri

The apartment was my idea.

So was the divorce.

And as our thirty-year relationship falls apart, my kids' father and I agree on absolutely nothing. Except this. Our three teenage kids will stay in their home full-time. The kids' father will also live there in an apartment attached to the main house. We will navigate our post-divorce lives around this premise.

Do not be misled by this decision. It is not an amicable divorce. There is bitterness and bleeding. Anger and distrust. But on this one concept, we ultimately agree and when we submit the paperwork to a judge for signature, the judge and her law clerk applaud our creativity.

They are the only ones.

Even the kids question me as the weeks and months go by and they try to explain our unusual living situation to friends. One day, my son tells me he's embarrassed to tell his new girlfriend about it, and he asks, "Why didn't you just have an ordinary divorce?"

There is, of course, nothing ordinary about our lives after the divorce. Their father and I are both healing, both moving on, and both still living at the same address. I can't speak for him, but for me, trying to heal from a broken marriage is excruciating with him nearby. I hear him sometimes through the walls talking about me. Saying things I should never have to hear.

He comes and goes freely from the apartment, with only a limited custody agreement tethering him to the space. I find myself breathing most easily when he's not around, but the kids gradually fall into a rhythm of wanting him around more often. They are forming their first real relationship with him following the divorce. It's what I'd hoped for. It's why I formulated this arrangement in the first place. And it's working. For them.

I talk to my therapist. To friends and family. No one understands why I am doing this.

This is not normal, they say. This is not what people do.

I know that, of course. I'm not trying to convince anyone otherwise. I'm trying to raise extraordinary children, and I'm trying to have an extraordinary life. My children move freely between the apartment and the main house. They sleep in their own beds every night and they never wonder whose house they will be in, even though their parents are divorced. The months go by, and we settle into a new normal. I've been dating fairly ordinary men, but suddenly I find myself wishing for something more. Something out of the ordinary.

I start sharing more of my story with men. More about my living situation. I go on second dates and third. I meet children. I am one guy's emergency contact when he has back surgery. Most men say my living situation isn't a problem, but no one really seems to understand it. Three years after the divorce, I still haven't found anyone who lights me up or sees me or understands me.

And yet, because of the living situation, and in spite of the divorce, I see my children thrive and heal and stop questioning why their parents chose to do something so unusual. Unlike so many "ordinary" couples I watch around me, I'm not staying in a failed marriage just for the kids. I'm not dying inside. My soul is ignited.

And while it's true that my ignited soul seems to be appreciated by no one other than, well, *me*, I enjoy myself. I travel alone to beautiful places from Sedona to Italy. I start a new career in nonprofit, and my budding writing career takes off. I realize one day, sitting on a beach in Miami on a solo vacation, with a glass of wine and my laptop, far from home—a home I share with my children and my ex-husband—that I am more alive than I've ever been and it doesn't matter that no one else is here to see it. I settle into my life. I thank the universe and my own gutsy refusal to settle for anything ordinary.

And then.

One day, I meet a man online who wants to take me on a first date. He has kind blue eyes, a warm smile, and he loves his teenage boys in a way that seems genuine and familiar to me. I agree to drinks, maybe dinner. I'm not sure anymore that I want anything other than me, my kids, and this life.

The day before our date, he texts me: *There's something I want to tell you. Something I feel like you should know before we go out. I have a very unusual living arrangement with my kids' mom,* he says, *something no one quite understands . . .*

I smile then at my phone, at the universe, at karma, and at the long and winding road I've been on that has brought me exactly to this place.

I text him that we'll have a lot to discuss over drinks. And as I hit send, I feel something that is not normal. I feel oddly, and finally . . . something that is *extraordinary.*

IT'S SAID THERE ARE AN EXTRAORDINARY AMOUNT OF FISH IN THE SEA. FIND THE 7 LOVENOTES! FISH

THE SECOND TIME AROUND
IT TAKES SOME COFFEE

Stacy Smith Rogers & Sara Stansberry

(As told by two friends in the
LoveNotes! Off-Broadway World Premiere February 10, 2024)

SARA: Well, it started with an email I didn't read. And a Bumble account I thought I'd deleted.

STACY: For me, it was a text from an unfamiliar number, asking if I'd be at my coffee shop on Thursday.

SARA: Yes, the universe usually has coffee involved in these "things."

STACY: Agreed.

SARA: It was June in North Carolina. I had completely unplugged in my family's remote cabin after dropping my daughter at camp. Anyway, I had deleted all my dating app accounts, exhausted by the online process. I was happily single. Divorced five years with three kids, I was figuring out how to do life on my own, working on myself, and reading books about healthy love *even* if I wasn't quite sure how to execute it in real life.

STACY: Five minutes before "the text," I had signed the papers ending my twenty-eight-year marriage, making me the sole owner of the coffee shop my husband and I had opened **six months** before the pandemic. He dropped the divorce bomb on February 9, and I was still numb from it all. I responded to the text with, *"May I ask who this is?"*

SARA: My email read, "Hi, I'm in Orlando this week, and your picture came up on my Bumble account. I don't fully understand how this works and didn't know if I should swipe left or right, so I am sending this email instead since we know each other already."

What? My Bumble account?

The words continued, "I'm in town until Sunday. I've read your blog and think we might have some things in common. Would you be interested in coffee or lunch? Walter"

STACY: "It's Chris,' my text said. Chris was the boy who had taken me to my senior prom a thousand years ago, who used to write me poems, whose shoulders I straddled at the Cheap Trick concert. He was my high school hottie who would hold me at my doorstep until the lights flickered, reminding me I was past curfew.

SARA: Walter was the kid at the bus stop thirty years ago. We'd been steps away from one another for most of our childhoods. We lived in the same Orlando neighborhood, eight houses apart, and rode the same bus each morning. He was a grade ahead of me, but I didn't know him that well.

And apparently, my face was somehow still floating around in Bumble cyberspace.

STACY: Thursday arrived. My barista was handing Chris his mocha when I first spotted him. That familiar jaw line. Those deep middle-of-the-ocean blue eyes. I wondered if he noticed the grief-ridden bags under mine, or my naked ring finger.

SARA: Three weeks earlier, I'd compiled an affirmation of sorts. A "Love Note" I'd written in the notes section on my phone.

I was trying to set an intention and focus on what I wanted out of life.

(looking at phone)

A man who sees me; who gets me; who knows me and wants to know more; a man who is there; who can just be with me because it's what he wants, because it's what I want. Together. A man who is supportive; who lives an exciting life; who will build an even more exciting one with me. A man who is sexy; who is confident; who loves making love to me and vice versa.

STACY: "You look great," Chris said. I almost believed him. For a few seconds, I was seventeen years old again. Being divorced too, he had walked his own "unhappily-ever-after" and he offered to guide me if I needed him.

I did need him.

SARA: Walter had sent the email almost five days prior. Was it too late to respond? Did I even want to? Nevertheless, I told him I could do coffee on Saturday.

STACY: Chris and I talked on the phone for hours. Not Face-Time. Just the *old-fashioned* kind of conversations like we used to have in high school late at night. Only now I'm whispering because of my kids in the next room, instead of my parents.

SARA: Somehow, coffee turned into lunch. Eleven hours later, he drove me home. He didn't kiss me or ask to "come in" when the night ended. As I got out of the car, he said, "I wanted to see if you were the person I'd been reading, if that person is really you."

"Well, it is," I said. "I don't know how to be any other way."

STACY: We talked about how debilitating divorce can be. Eventually, I invited him over for dinner and he told me, "I always thought that if I died, I would want you to know that I never forgot you. And that I have always had you in my heart."

We stared at each other for a long time. I reached out first. There was no curfew that night.

SARA: Walter lived in Las Vegas, and I was in Orlando. There were lots of endless phone conversations at night and plenty of Starbucks door dashes in the morning with, "Sorry I kept you up so late." We were smitten.

STACY: Chris and I fall into Round #2 of boyfriend/girlfriend. But my wounds are still too fresh and I let New Year's Eve pass alone on my couch. The February 9 anniversary of the divorce bomb is hanging in front of me like a *scorched latte*. The only thing I can do is write.

SARA: One day, Walter paused on the phone and said, "I know it's early, and I hate to do this over the phone, but I want to tell you, I think I'm in love with you." And because it felt like the most natural thing in the world, I said, "Me too."

STACY: Words tumbled onto my keyboard at record speed for weeks. When I finally closed my laptop on February 9, I received a text.

It read: *I love you. A new year starts tomorrow.*

I knew the number. I knew the man sending it. He knew me. And my New Year, my new life, began with this text.

SARA: I told Walter I fell in love with his heart. He said he fell in love with my mind.

You know, Stacy, today is February 10.

STACY: That's right. It's my New Year's Day—the day I traded ashes for confetti.

SARA: Let's celebrate with a cup of coffee.

L♥VE✉NOTES!

STACY: Here's to love.

(the women clink rhinestone bedazzled coffee mugs)

"If at first you don't succeed,
try, try again."

ROBERT THE BRUCE

THIRD TIME'S A CHARM

Wanda Colón

I met the love of my life and now husband, Rich, thirty years ago. We joke that our first date was with other people. He was with another woman, a cute blond, sitting at the bar in Fegley's Restaurant when I walked in with my then-boyfriend, David, who would become my first husband. Unbeknownst to me, Rich and David were best friends.

Rich and I crossed paths over the years, but we were always attached to other people. I went to his second wedding, and he attended my first. We double-dated all the time—me with David and Rich with another blond who became his second wife.

There was the James Taylor concert in Philadelphia when I first saw Rich in shorts.

"Wow, nice legs there," I joked (but wasn't really kidding). Rich's wife didn't appreciate my comment.

And Rich reminds me that we first saw *The Phantom of the Opera* together, but it was with other people, of course. Ever the romantic and a theater major, I cried for the Phantom and Christine as I so wanted them to end up together. Decades later, Rich told me he'd secretly watched me weep and it had touched him in a way that he didn't know what to make of it.

"Uh-huh, you loved me back then, didn't you?" I laughed. I knew he thought I was hot even if we were off-limits to each other. He never would have broken the man code.

I was happy enough with David and excited about moving to Los Angeles to pursue my acting and TV hosting career. I grew up in a family where men cheated and women put up with it, so I felt lucky that David was loyal and we loved each other. Until one day, when I innocently checked my emails on David's laptop and discovered he was living a secret life and having affairs with several women simultaneously. My heart stopped and my stomach sank; I was devastated and blindsided. Betrayed. There was no way I could stay with this man.

Within a couple of weeks, I went from being a happily married wife to sitting in an empty apartment with only a coffee table and a bed. Husband number one was history!

Money was tight, so I went on audition after audition, and received rejection after rejection, until I finally booked a "modeling job" that paid $1,000, plus tip. Then it hit me—the gig was for an escort service. Oh jeez! What would I have to do for the tip? I was desperate and my rent was due, so I hightailed it to church and prayed on it. That night, I lay awake all night, tossing and turning with visions of my mom telling her friends back in Pennsylvania that I'd become a hooker in LA. I didn't take the job, but between us I kept the number just in case.

Well, God must have been listening, because a couple of days later I booked a GMC commercial, which saved me—I didn't have to cry *mercy* and go home. (Sidenote, I am still the proud owner of a GMC.) That advertisement was the catalyst that led me to host HGTV's *24 Hour Design* for four seasons and later *Home Made Simple for Six*, where I met my second husband.

He was tall with green eyes, and in charge as the Director of Photography. He swept me off my feet in a whirlwind, doing everything to win me over. Romantic out-of-the-box excursions—like private chef dinners, intimate tours of the Empire State Building, and more. But he also did everything to lose me, like two-week silence treatments and making me feel guilty for becoming ill. After seven long years, and two bouts with breast cancer, I was beat up and couldn't take it anymore. I left, vowing to never love again. Done with Number Two!

After twenty years in LA, I moved home to Pennsylvania, and was there for about a minute when I ran into my first husband's best friend, Rich, at the local Beverly Hills Tavern. We hadn't seen each other in fifteen years, but soon discovered we were both divorced and that he was no longer in touch with husband number one. The liquid courage was running through my veins, and after finishing my third glass of wine, we locked gazes.

"Wow, you have beautiful eyes," he said.

I dove in and kissed him, biting his lip so hard he checked for blood. I honestly wanted to hook up, but he drove me home, tenderly kissed me goodnight, and insisted on asking me out on a proper date.

There was a small obstacle—he lived in Florida.

Nevertheless, we planned a two-week, get-reacquainted visit in the Sunshine State. I landed at Tampa International Airport on Valentine's Day 2020. Covid canceled my return flight. And well, I never left. We married a year later.

I guess it's true—third time's a charm!

Love is sometimes a game of numbers!

FILL IN THE MISSING NUMBERS

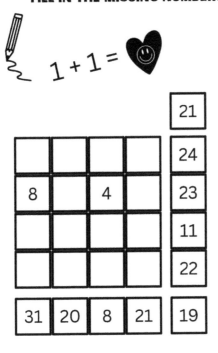

- The missing numbers are integers between 0 and 10.
- The numbers in each row add up to totals to the right.
- The numbers in each column add up to totals along the bottom.
- The diagonal lines also add up to totals on the right.

EVERY WORD IS TRUE

Kay Stephens

I was nearly forty when I first fell in love. Now, don't get me wrong, I had an adventurous first four decades in the romance department. I dated my way across the globe, had been engaged (twice!), and one of those engagements even turned into a ten-year marriage. But I had never known that earth-shattering, head-over-heels love described in romance novels. And, to be honest, after half a lifetime I thought that type of love was a farce—nothing more than an illusion manufactured by romance authors and sold by the wedding industry.

But in the sad, failing days of my first marriage, I decided if the love illusion was as close as I could get, I might as well chase it as one of those misinformed romance authors. I poured my life's resentments into drafting a novel—working after work, sleeping two or three hours on my best nights, and writing until my fingers ached and my brain cramped. And I ended up with a three-hundred-page book that was nothing short of horrendous. It lacked heart, it lacked soul, and it lacked any sort of realism inherent in the world's greatest love stories. Seriously, it was one of the worst pieces of American literature ever written.

If there was one beautiful thing that came from that ugly book, though, it was a character named James. He was a blond-haired, blue-eyed, potty-mouthed military man who loved love and hated social conformity. A sexual renegade, my imaginary readers may have thought—economy-size box of condoms and broken headboard included with purchase. And I became obsessed with that character, writing and rewriting him until he was the prototype of a person I could fall in love with—at least in that fairy-tale world where romantic love actually existed.

Well, to the surprise of no one, my first attempt at writing failed miserably. No agent or publishing house wanted to look at me, let alone work with me. Even my editor sent the book back with notes that can be summarized into one simple question: "What is this?"

After taking several months to heal from the rejection of both author failure and divorce, I sought out mentors to teach me how to write and therapists to teach me how to date. I spent my days searching for my next ex-spouse, dating jet-setting pilots, successful business owners, and even a hot retired football player. People who would have been perfect for almost anyone, really, except this girl who could only seem to fall for a fictional character.

At night I began working on a second attempt at a novel, which looked nothing like the first other than that blond-haired, potty-mouthed military man—James, the character I could never seem to walk away from. The book was still overwritten and about twenty thousand words too long for a marketable romance novel, but it was better. I was getting better.

And then, one day, a friend sent that simple five-word text that alters realities—*I found someone for you.* I can't quite remember what the follow-up text said, but the description went something like, *He's a blond-haired, blue-eyed military veteran. He's a bit of a non-conformist but a lot of fun. And you might want to reinforce your headboard.* In short, he was James—the James I had created. My James had emerged from the pages of my terrible romance novel and dropped into my real world.

My real-life James promised me nothing but gave me everything. He was the one who convinced me that our love, not financial success, was our greatest life adventure. He was the one who pulled my second novel off the shelf, handed it to me, and said, "Let's get this thing published." That book was just released for sale and, yes, I'm proud to announce my fictional James actually made it through final edits.

If you are a love-denier like I was, please continue to suspend your disbelief for just another moment. Step into your imagination and begin to create your true love. Hell, jot them down in a book if you need to. Just never allow your soul to accept the lie that romantic love is an illusion. It took me four decades, a divorce, and the world's worst romance novel to realize it, but I promise you that true love is real and it is life-changing. Now go out and write it for yourself.

If you could write your perfect partner into existence, describe what that person would be like.

EVERYBODY HAS A MATCH.

Find the Cupid couples.

THE DANCE (FOR V.C.)

Karen Rippstein

In 1993, we sing along

to the Bangles' *Eternal Flame.*

Become lovers midway

between your medical residency

my birthday and a delirious

night of dancing.

Your tall frame leans

into me like a magnet.

We rock to the beat

of Blondie's *Rapture*

my request the DJ plays.

Your hands grab my hips,

our steps in sync.

We entwine for Journey's *Open Arms*

and Annie Lenox's *Why*.

Lips touch for the igniting kiss.

L♥VE✉NOTES!

Passion explodes,

the dance continues

between New York and California.

You want me for your wife

it's easier being your friend.

I send you lyrics

to Wilson Phillips' *Release Me.*

New York is my home

I still dance there.

"New York City is always hopeful.
Always it believes that something good
is about to happen, and it must
hurry to meet it."

UNKNOWN

LAST STAND

Haley Lawrence

D ear S—,

It was a dreary wet December morning when your friend Michael phoned from Newark Airport to announce he and his five English mates had landed and were ready to paint New York City red. I was shocked. I'd run into Michael at a night out in Roppongi, Tokyo a few weeks prior. Truth is, I didn't even recall giving him my number.

As a single New Yorker, thirty-eight years old and perpetually single, I was finally at peace with the idea that marriage and kids were not in my future. My life was good—I'd recently closed on my second apartment, my new coaching career was exploding, and my consulting business had me hopscotching around the world.

"Julie, let's go," I announced to my anything-goes French-Canadian girlfriend. Dressed in five-inch heels and miniskirts with a small stash of mood-altering substances in hand, we headed off into a wild weekend with your band of hard-partying Brits. One that cataclysmically ended, if you remember, with your thrill-seeking (not so smart) spontaneous friend, Oliver, jumping off my balcony and breaking both of his ankles.

If I'm honest, I thought you were a one-night stand. Okay, maybe a two-moons fling. Five years younger than me and living on the other side of the world, you weren't what I imagined as relationship material. It had been a fun weekend, and that was it. We kissed goodbye on 103rd Street and I waved to you, watching the yellow taxi's red brake lights fade into the city traffic. *Well, that was fun,* I thought with a smile, but without a second thought.

Apparently, you had other plans. And it didn't matter that there was an ocean between us. By August we were married and London became our home.

Two beautiful daughters, a couple of dogs, four cats, six houses, twenty-three countries, several businesses, lots of jobs, and twenty-five years later we're still going strong.

What began as an impromptu night turned into the most important relationship of my life.

It's said everything can change in a day. And we're living proof that's true. Here's to another quarter century together. Cheers!

With love,

H.

SERENDIPITY
AND THE CITY

Melissa Giberson

The thought of dating after being married for nineteen years opened a Pandora's Box of mixed emotions running the gamut from euphoria to fear.

I had limited dating experience; I'd been in a relationship with my ex-husband since age twenty-one. Yet this paled in comparison to the significant challenge of seeking companionship in an entirely different demographic. I went from being a straight, married, suburban New Jersey mom to understanding I was a forty-something lesbian with no clue about dating, let alone dating women!

Meeting prospective romantic partners meant showing up where interesting people might be, Meetup groups, and the most angst-filled option—online dating. Stretching outside my comfort zone, this introvert traveled hours to find other gay women. A wardrobe update to one better suited for dating in my new sexual orientation included new shirts, jeans, Converse sneakers, and cowboy boots. I found myself playing flag football on the Jersey Shore, ferrying to Fire Island, hanging out with kindred late gay-bloomers in Connecticut, visiting queer bars in Philadelphia, driving to Provincetown multiple times, hiking, biking, partaking in trivia nights, attending dances where I was the youngest person in the room, and events where I was the oldest. I commuted in and out of Manhattan so much I should have had my own tube for the Lincoln Tunnel.

Life-long lesbians called me taboo, saying women would run from me, and advised me to go back to my safe straight life—that newbie, middle-aged lesbianism was too hard.

I remained steadfast, but concerned I'd never meet anyone. Encounters with women from the Midwest, California, the East Coast, and Canada left me wondering how this single mom could manage a long-distance relationship considering time constraints. Plus, there was the added challenge of rediscovering one's sexuality in her fifth decade. It's like going through a second adolescence.

Online dating was no better. It yielded localized brow-raising moments, including women trolling the sites looking for sex and women seeking a third to join their boyfriend or husband. A woman with a Cheshire cat grin looked adoringly at me across the bistro table and declared it was destiny because of our shared Jewish lineage. The cute British DJ on the rebound was intriguing until I learned that she and her ex still lived together and shared custody of a cat named Beau. One woman met me in SoHo and reported finishing a bottle of wine before our date. She shared a story of being so drunk once that she forgot where she parked her car only to discover a year later that it had been impounded. Real winners I was finding. Then there was the lawyer, determined to be in a committed relationship before her fortieth birthday, who courted me with titillating emails of our imagined sexual encounters. The one-and-done dates were racking up, and it seemed the only female I'd be cuddling with in my future was my cat.

My Later In Life Meetup group hosted a dinner in the West Village. While I opted out, my curiosity led me there just as women were leaving. A stunning, tall, dark-haired woman walked past me, sparking a pang of regret for not attending.

But life went on. That summer, my kids and I visited gay-friendly Rehoboth Beach. My eleven-year-old son boogie-boarded with Brenda, a forty-something single woman he met on the lesbian beach, while I chatted with two moms and their one-year-old baby. Compared to my former life, things couldn't be more upside down.

The next Later In Life Meetup dinner event rolled around. *Should I go?* The treks into Manhattan were exhausting and expensive. But hope springs eternal, so I sent the kids to my mom's and donned my newest white V-neck tee, faded blue jeans, and flip-flops to show off my sorbet-painted toenails. Still, my ambivalence about attending increased the longer I sat in tunnel and city street traffic. *Am I a masochist?* After circling the Chelsea streets countless times, I pulled over to ponder whether not finding parking was a sign to cut my losses and go home. Then a black car pulled away across the street, and I decided *that* was my sign—I was supposed to attend the dinner. I slipped into the space and nervously checked my face in the rearview mirror. The restaurant was a cool two-story converted taxi garage.

A half dozen women sat around a banquette awkwardly chatting. One woman refused to give her real name at the check-in table, and I wondered why she bothered to come. *Was this a mistake? What movie was I missing on the TCM channel?*

Then, as if in a Hollywood scene, a woman who looked like a model walked toward our table, her long brown hair flowing like a gentle breeze. Everyone and everything else faded away. When she slid onto the bench seat across from me, I had my sign. Her name was Vivian and I spent the rest of the night trying to talk to her.

Vivian realized her authentic sexuality ten years earlier, but this was only the second event she had ever attended. The first was the dinner I had skipped a few months back. *She* was the woman who had walked past me. Vivian admitted she almost didn't come into the restaurant—frustrated by the long drive and the parking challenge. She sat in her car crying before deciding to join the dinner.

When the night ended, I offered her my number and said, "If you ever feel like getting a drink." After all, Vivian lived a mere twenty minutes from my house in the suburbs—perhaps another sign.

Soon, the text on my flip phone read, "Do you still want to get a drink?"

Ten years later, it's part history and part serendipity. Today we share a home in New Jersey and visit the city together.

THE BENCH

Johanne Pelletier

She has a brain tumor and it's serious. And we are all here—family, friends, friends of friends—all of us have traveled from afar to New York City, where she lives, for her surgery.

She is my ex, Angie, a recent ending after five years of being in a long-distance relationship. We tried but the almost constant travel, exciting at first, had no end in sight for us. The whole thing was and still is complicated. We remain in touch, still close emotionally, and trying to find a friendship growing beyond where we were.

I want to be here because I care very much but I don't want to intrude, or assume this is my place. We discuss it and she insists I come. She says whatever we are now, you are always family. You have to come. I don't know how much I am regarded as family or if this is the fear of the surgery talking, but I agree to come.

My flight arrives on a frigid cold January day and despite the chill I am sweaty and nervous heading to one of those Pod hotels. Sure, I care a lot, but I think this trip could be a mistake. Her family was never entirely accepting of her decision to be in a relationship with a woman. She tells me it is cultural and perhaps what saved us the awkwardness of family encounters is that they live in another part of the world.

The night before the surgery, there is a group dinner attended by all the family, friends, and friends of friends, and there is disagreement about who should be at the hospital for the surgery the next morning.

Angie leans over and whispers to me, "Please, I need you there, please come."

Her family feels differently, declaring their wish for only family at the hospital. They can handle it all, they say. They will alert us after the surgery. I head back to my hotel and leave them at the restaurant arguing.

I would love to call friends at home to share this weird, awkward dinner with them. But it's too late to call and I know my friends didn't think I should be here anyway. Nothing about this trip feels right. I wish I had listened to friends, listened to my gut, and stayed home. I did not need to be here to care.

My ex, my friend, Angie, I am not sure what to call her anymore, phones me late that night after the dinner, pleading, "Never mind my family, they are worried and stressed, listen to me, please come to the hospital tomorrow morning."

The next morning I meet her in the hotel lobby with her family. There are friends, and friends of friends here too, and the tension and stress of the night before has eased. Angie is happy to see me, and we all walk to Sloan Kettering Cancer Center together talking, laughing, distracting ourselves and her.

The ease is short-lived because once she goes into surgery her family pulls me aside to say, "It is nice you are here, but you can take a break now, we've got this. Why not take a walk in the city, go shopping. Someone will call you later."

So now I leave the hospital and wander to Central Park, pensive and worried.

I come across benches with sponsored plaques on them. I stop at one that says *love all, trust a few, do harm to none*. Wow, how I love this, because this is what I really believe and how I try to live. I am a messy mix of emotion, exhaustion, and stress about this trip, about the uncertainty of being here, and I am worried about her, the surgery, hoping she will be okay. Something about this bench calms me, like the one thing that makes sense to me so far in this trip. I post a photo of the plaque on Instagram with the tags #loveall, #prayers, and #getbetter. I am sending out positive vibes, hoping she will survive.

And it starts, notifications on Instagram, and then a private message from someone I don't know, another *she*, a hatmaker in Germany. This stranger tells me how well she knows my ex. She knows a lot about me too. She is sorry to reach out, but she has nobody else to ask. She is desperate for news about the surgery. She writes, "How is my sweetheart, my longtime love?"

Sweetheart? I have never heard of this woman.

"Wait, who are you?" I message. She doesn't answer.

And now the phone rings; it is friends at the hospital telling me to return. I sprint back. The surgery went well, Angie is fine, and the prognosis is good. Her family invites me to dinner, but I tell them I might join later.

I watch her sleep from a distant chair in her room. I am grateful she is okay, but I am also numb, tired, replaying the day, trying to make sense of why I came here. And what do I do with the hatmaker messages?

And what about the bench and that phrase, *love all, trust a few, do harm to none?* I believe this but now I am unsure about loving all, and less sure I even trust a few. I hope I've done no harm.

It is complicated. The trip was a mistake but I am glad to have come, glad Angie is okay. We are exes and maybe friends. Maybe we will remain close but, no, we are not really family.

And I have many questions, but I cannot ask any of them now. I do not think I ever will. I stay awhile in her room and leave on an early flight the next morning.

DEPARTURES IN THE RAIN

Joe Farina

almost broke down

almost spoke your name

she was on the crosstown bus

wearing her hair like yours

stopped at erie and ouelette

as i walked by one misted night

in windsor under a winter rain—

she was sitting by the window

half obscured by condensation

her breath visible like filaments of cloud

the dull bus light shadowing her eyes

i turned to search her face

but she disappeared into the cold mist

like you did so long ago . . .

and though i wanted to forget you

i still whispered to your shadows

NAME THE CODE & MESSAGE

.. / .-.. --- ...- . / -.-- --- ..-

Code:_____. Message:_____

01001001 00100000 01101100 01101111
01110110 01100101 00100000 01111001
01101111 01110101

Code:_____. Message:_____

143

Code:_____. Message:_____

TIMING

Ronna J. Levy

I'm teaching English and public speaking to ninth and tenth graders at a high school in Hell's Kitchen. Hell's Kitchen—before it became "Brunch Kitchen." This is my first teaching job, and Lee, a veteran teacher, is my mentor. Lee is patient and caring. He shows me how to write a lesson plan, manage my classroom, and basically how to teach. Sometimes, after we finish working on my lessons, we sit and talk. Lee tells me about his time in the Peace Corps, movies he's seen, restaurants he likes. He's so interesting and comfortable to be with. He's a good listener and genuinely interested in my life. I feel special and safe. I get butterflies when I see him.

But then I start thinking: Lee is twelve years older than I. He's a vegetarian; I eat burgers. He lives in suburban New Jersey; I'm in Manhattan. And, he has a thirteen-year-old son he sees every other weekend. He's settled in a regular life with a career, house, car, kid. He's everything I'm not. He's everything I don't want. I don't want a regular life. I want a creative life as a writer, an actress. Teaching is simply a stop along the way as I figure things out.

But I really enjoy being with Lee. Soon enough, we start dating. Damn, we are so good together. We see movies, ride bikes, make dinners, play Scrabble. We date through the school year, through the summer, and into the fall. That autumn, however, I stop teaching and begin grad school at Brooklyn College, taking poetry with Allen Ginsberg, acting with F. Murray Abraham. I am on my creative way.

One afternoon, Lee leaves a message on my answering machine. He invites me to Rosh Hashanah dinner to meet his mother. I hear "meet my mother," and I think, *I'm not ready for anyone's mother*. This is too fast, too serious. So, I do what I do when I don't know what to do. I disappear. I ignore his message, and don't call him back. I know I am hurting a kind and generous man, but I'm not ready. And I go on with my life.

Four years later, in June, Lee calls and invites me to a retirement lunch for a colleague. It's nice hearing his voice. He tells me that it will be lovely to see me and catch up. Then he adds, "I miss you." I hear, "I miss you," and in my immaturity and insecurity my mind jumps to "meet my mother," and I'm not sure I want to go with him to this luncheon. But then I remind myself: I'm moving to Los Angeles in two months to be in a friend's movie. My creative life is across the country. So, I go to the luncheon, and without missing a beat, we get back together. It's so easy to be with Lee. But I'm still going to LA to start a new life.

Before I leave, Lee asks for my picture and resume. He wants to pin it on the bulletin board in his home office. He wants to see my smile every day. Then he says he'll wait for me. I feel terrible and guilty and think: *Please don't wait for me. I'm not coming back!*

I move to LA. Soon, Lee and I start writing letters. He types long, single-spaced letters about the high school, movies he's seen, and camping trips he's taken. Lee's last paragraphs are emotional; he misses me and hopes someday we can be together. But then he always adds a few sentences apologizing for getting too personal. He knows I'll disappear. But I like his emotional paragraphs. I miss him.

Working on the movie is fun and I'm in a theater company and do some plays, but I'm also waitressing, working in a production office, and of all things, I'm teaching in a community college. I thought I left teaching in New York. And while I'm in LA, my brother gets married and has a baby, my sister's kids are growing up, my dad needs a heart valve replacement and is diagnosed with leukemia, my grandfather dies and I miss the funeral.

Why am I in LA?

It's Y2K, new beginnings. I return to New York. And once again, without missing a beat, Lee and I get back together. This time for keeps.

One Sunday morning we're walking back to my apartment from Starbucks. Lee tells me to think about what furniture I might want from his house. An odd request. But wait, this must mean we're getting an apartment together. Of course! He can't take all the furniture from his house, so what would I like to have in our new apartment? I do an inventory of his furniture. Then he tells me that the year before I came back to New York, he'd been diagnosed with metastatic melanoma. He did research—there is no cure; he's going to let the cancer take its course.

My stomach drops, my tongue ties, my heart breaks.

We don't know how much time we have. I meet his mother and we all go to Paris together. I meet his son and we all go camping in Wyoming. Lee meets my family on Thanksgiving. He smokes cigars and drinks whiskey with my brother and plays guitar with my nephew. We see movies, make dinners, ride bikes, play Scrabble.

For the next five years, we live.

We. Live.

Until we can't.

"Though nothing can bring back the hour of splendor in the grass, of glory in the flower; We will grieve not, rather find strength in what remains behind."

WILLIAM WORDSWORTH

ABOUT LOVE

Kerri Quinn

It was June, the second time I moved to New York, and I was living in a sublet near the West Village. Between writing and looking for jobs and friends, I roamed. While the rest of Manhattan wore sandals, shorts, and flowery dresses, I—dressed in my writer's outfit of running tights, a rainbow-colored knit hat, a coffee-stained sweatshirt, and a long black sweater with one pocket hanging off—looked like the lone survivor of the apocalypse.

One afternoon, while looking for friends, I followed two men to the corner of Seventh Avenue and Fourteenth Street. They wore matching skinny jeans, white shirts, and black suspenders. I leaned into the shorter man, sniffed his shoulder.

"Can I help you?" he asked.

"What kind of detergent do you use?" I asked.

His friend rolled his eyes at me.

"You smell like my boyfriend, Sid," I said.

"The one that left you because you're crazy?" The friend eyed my outfit. I eyed *his* in return.

The light changed. The shorter man said, "Tide Simply Clean and Fresh," and walked away.

On my way back to the apartment, I bought a bottle of Tide. My neighbor, Biceps, the man with the tattooed bulging arms whose name I could never remember, sat on the stoop, talking on the phone. As I climbed the steps, he squeezed my hand. It was the first time in months someone had touched me and it took my breath away. His eyes were watery and so were mine. I went into the apartment and opened the window. I felt guilty for eavesdropping, but I was so tired of being alone.

"I'm old enough to be your father," Biceps said.

A police car raced down the street. Flashing red lights filled the room.

"You said it was okay," he said.

I went to the bathroom, filled the sink, poured in some detergent, and inhaled. It didn't smell like Sid.

*

Ten days after Sid hit a deer going seventy miles per hour on his motorcycle, I sat outside his ICU room with Michael, a representative from the Arizona Donor Network, and Sid's father, Norman.

"His eyes? Skin?" Michael asked.

We had already said yes to donating Sid's liver and kidneys.

"He has the prettiest hazel eyes," Norman said.

Michael repeated the question. Norman and I nodded yes.

*

It was September; I was still jobless and time was running out on my sublet. Somehow, I let my mother convince me to go to Lake George with her and my step-father, Don, for their twenty-sixth wedding anniversary.

Before the three of us, the parents and the child, went to dinner, we stood in the kitchen, our glasses filled with champagne.

"Thanks for taking me on your anniversary trip," I said. "Here's to twenty-six more years."

"Only twenty-six?" my mother said.

"I want fifty more," Don said.

*

The night before the accident, Sid and I stood on the side of the Grand Canyon and he asked me to marry him. The moon was round and bright. A circle of stars hung below it like a strand of pearls. Before I could answer, he told me he wanted to ask me again, to make it special. I looked up at the moon, at the shining, pearl-like stars and thought, this is pretty darn special. That was eleven years ago.

*

It was October, I was still jobless and my sublet was up, so I decided to go back to Arizona. The day before I left, I ran into Biceps on the stoop. Dressed in my apocalyptic writer's outfit, I sat down and told him I was leaving New York. Again. He told me that his boyfriend broke up with him. Again. A man in a yellow raincoat walking a schnauzer wearing a matching raincoat stopped in front of us.

"I should have this guy dress me," I said.

"You should." Biceps laughed.

*

The night before Sid was taken off life support, I went to his hospital room. His hands were swollen and shaped like oven mitts. The monitors beeped. A respirator, the size of a small refrigerator, shook his body.

"You can wake up now," I said and lay on the bed next to him, my head on his chest.

The next morning, as the doctor removed the breathing tube, I held Sid's hand, and his mother held the other. A few minutes later, he was gone.

The doctor moved me aside so the medical team could wheel Sid out of the room. They had five minutes before his organs would begin to fail. Sid's mother fainted. A nurse rushed in with a wheelchair and whisked her away. And I stood there, in the empty room, the respirator, the monitors gone, and I opened my mouth but no sounds, no words came out.

The night before he died, I promised him that I would always be his friend, that I would never forget him. As I lay next to him, my head on his chest, I knew he heard me.

AGREE OR DISAGREE?

CRACK THE CODE & CIRCLE

YES OR NO

A	B	C	D	E	F	G	H
	G						

I	J	K	L	M	N	O	P	Q
						L		

R	S	T	U	V	W	X	Y	Z
S								

```
_ _ _     B _ _ _ _ R   _ O     _ _ _ _   _ O _ _ _   _ _ _
K D A     G T K K T S   K L     B O W T   J L W T Y   O M Y

_ O _ _   _ _ _ _     _ _ _ _ R   _ O   _ _ _ _   _ O _ _
J L A K   K B O M     M T W T S   K L   B O W T   J L W T Y

              _ _   _ _ _ .
              O K   O J J
```

EXTRA LOVE CREDIT:

WHO SAID THIS? _____

95

Endings can be slow and drawn out or incredibly abrupt. We often do not know a last encounter is the final interaction with a lover. Think about one such situation. What would you say or do now, knowing you would never see that person again?

TREE

Deborah Grey

That tree. The oak to the left of the old stone church. That big fucking tree with the roots twisting out of the ground in a bifurcated formation that appeared as legs if you looked at it head-on or a tentacle if you came at it from behind the rectory. You know which one I mean, the one with the bark as thick as a palm and crusty like a good Italian bread. Like the one we bought at the San Gennaro festival with some olives and a stretch of sausage and ate it in your car behind the church. Remember? When you spilled the olive oil all over your hand and I wiped it clean with a hunk of bread you broke off for me. And then I ate it—I ate the bread—and you laughed like crazy. That's when I knew I really loved you.

That tree. Where you took me for the last time. Rather, we took each other, knowing it was goodbye. I lay on my back with those gnarly wooden knuckles pressing into my spine and let you ravage me for what I knew was the ending. The pain was excruciating but the sky through the tree's branches was an analgesic. The stars twinkled, as stars do, and the moon looked down in an accusatory way. "I'll give you tonight," it said, "but not a minute more. Go home to your life, your daylight life, and don't let me see you here again."

Several years later I saw on the news that the church burned down. It was a tremendous fire and took the one-hundred-year-old structure right down to the handlaid stone foundation. I no longer lived in town, but I found a reason to drive by the ashen remains. I parked my car in the empty, overgrown parking lot where weeds were eating away at the pavement. I got out and walked the perimeter, trying to understand how such a solid structure could be demolished in this way, and I sighed a little. To be honest, I sighed a lot. My steps followed the stone walkway from the rectory around to the side yard, looking for the tree, hoping it was still there.

In its fall splendor, that majestic tree stood tall, its branches arching over the fence that separated it from the building next door. Its boughs were filled with incendiary hues. The leaves formed mounds that crested one on top of the other like smoke plumes or cumulus clouds reaching toward heaven, fed by the wind and air beneath.

I rounded the tree several times, trying to locate just the right spot where I was rooted to that ground, that tree, you. I stretched out my hands to touch the bark, to run my fingers up and down its scaly skin. I tried to embrace it but my arms only made it halfway around. It had been growing fatter every year, one ring after another. One lover after another. It wouldn't stop just because we did. I was happy it had survived the fire.

DUAL PORTRAIT

David Masello

In an art school gallery of portraits depicting the same model, I chose to buy the one in which he is *not* seen. I was attending the weekly show of works at New York's Art Students League, and the largest wall of the exhibition space was filled to the ceiling with images of a lean, young man.

In most of the portraits on display, the model wears the white T-shirt and blue jeans he's donned for the sitting. Some students have him perched on a chair, or depict him standing, backdropped by a billowing curtain. He is positioned in profile in some canvases, in others, a distant, ancillary figure, and in still others, his face fills the frame.

In the portrait I now own, only parts of him are made visible—a gleaming silver belt buckle that reflects the open book he holds, his sinewy, hairless arms reaching into the foreground, veins forking across a hand, taught thighs swelling in jeans.

I confess to being attracted to portraits of handsome young men. I want pictures of beautiful faces and bodies on my walls—figures who never age like Dorian Grays, who remain forever available, who await me every day because I live with them. I keep this portrait unframed because I want no part of him omitted—a subtle strategy to offset the looming omission in my life of someone I'd come to love at the time I took possession of the work.

The painter, a diplomat's wife, wouldn't commit to a sale until she met me, to learn why I wanted her young man and where it is he might "live in my home," as she said to me prior to our meeting.

We met in a café on a blustery January Sunday. As I approached the corner, I saw her waiting, struggling to keep a giant Duane Reade plastic bag containing the painting from being buffeted by the wind. Once inside, she leaned it against her chair, not willing to relinquish it or even suggest it would become mine until I auditioned for the chance to own it.

"When I got the message that a stranger wanted to buy my painting," she said, "I was so excited that I called my husband in Singapore. No one before has ever bought a work of mine. I'll always remember this experience—because it's the first one."

The first one. That remark filled me with a sense of responsibility, an eerie echo of another responsibility I'd recently assumed. For a year, I'd been romantically involved with a much younger man. I'd not sought out someone nearly half my age and when we met, I tried to establish some emotional distance, refusing to believe that any such pairing was possible or appropriate. When this young man, Peter, announced to me one day that I was his first ever serious relationship, I felt elation—and dread.

"Whatever happens between us, no matter how long we're together, I'll never forget this," he said. "You'll always be my first boyfriend."

Unlike the painting of the young man I now own, a figure who will not age or leave my life, I knew that Peter would do both—moving abroad with a Fulbright and becoming immersed in a new canvas of friends, destinations, passions (academic and romantic ones). I never want to be that older man trying to hold the younger man in place; it's a most unflattering pose to assume. That is a portrait I never wish to own.

I know, too, that even if Peter and I had agreed to stay together, he would still be a youngish man as I age out of middle age. Math matters.

Perhaps the woman's portrait of a young man whom I imagine to be as attractive as Peter appealed to me so much because he is mine to keep as he exists. I knew that the figure in the painting would remain with me when Peter left New York for a life as a scholar-in-training and as an expatriate. His leaving would put an end to our midweek dinners and our weekend domestic routine, when he'd fill in the Sunday crossword as effortlessly as writing sentences.

At the café, the artist told me that she was the wife of a UN ambassador, having grown up in their small nation in a traditional Indian family, and had agreed to an arranged Hindu marriage. "I love my parents too much to have married, initially, for love," she told me when I asked, perhaps inappropriately, why someone so modern and young would adhere to such traditions. "I couldn't risk disappointing them."

Our cappuccinos finished and our conversation complete, I handed her an envelope of cash and she seemed embarrassed, as if the commerce associated with her art was something tawdry, a scenario she'd never envisioned upon completing the painting.

"It's yours now," she said, passing me the bag with an expression of both joy and wistfulness, for she was relinquishing something she'd made and might never see again. Perhaps she was thinking, "So, this is the price of doing good work that other people like—having to give it up."

The moment I gripped the bag, she said, "Maybe someday I could look at your collection of paintings," as a way to reassure herself that she might be seeing him again and how he was "living" where I lived.

After all, she loved her young man, too, and, as with me, the dual portraits we possessed were leaving us for destinations we would not be able to visit or in which we would live.

(NOT) MY PERSONAL JESUS

Julie Kling

M y first love was Jesus Christ. No, not anyone's Lord and Savior, but
the seventeen-year-old actor playing Jesus in a 1998 production of
Godspell at Stagedoor Manor. (That's upstate New York's *premier* teen
drama camp. Getting in only requires a financial audition from the parents,
but a young Natalie Portman attended for three days in 1996, so you know
it must also be very, very good.)

My Jesus had curly, sandpaper-colored hair that made him look like
the divine offspring of a Roman god and a sheep. He also had a facial
tick—if I said something filthy or honest or authentic to him, the entire
side of his face would spasm up and to the right, as if his skin was trying
to leap off his cheekbones. (We met when he was seventeen and I was
fourteen, so all was Kosher, but in a year, when he turned eighteen, our
love would become statutory.)

They cast fourteen-year-old me as Sonia, a.k.a. the embodiment of
Christ's temptation, and to our twenty-year-old choreographer Paolo fresh
out of NYU Tisch, "temptation" was best physicalized by me straddling
Jesus and riding him across the stage in every single scene. On show night,
I galloped past my horrified parents in the front row. Not only was their

daughter a divine sexpot, but she had also clearly spent her summer becoming a big Jew for Jesus.

Christ and I dated hot and heavy, albeit long distance, from ages sixteen to eighteen. (It's amazing to think back on the kind of emotional intimacy and burgeoning, fumbling sexual expression AOL Instant Messenger could facilitate, even in the days of dial-up.) And then, on my eighteenth birthday, he dumped me, which is young even by Leonardo DiCaprio's standards.

We had intermittent flings until I was twenty-five (Leonardo DiCaprio's actual standard). I'm almost forty now, and I still think about my personal Jesus more than I'd like to. In mundane moments of daily crisis with my young children, suburban sadness, or just feeling less than, I say his (real) name like an involuntary reflex—almost self-punishment. As an elder millennial woman cruelly subjected to '90s rom-com brainwashing, it's not all *that* surprising I believed I was destined for my first love. I thought we'd eventually stop dicking around, agree to spend our lives evolving together, and then one day, I'd throw on five hundred layers of silk taffeta to ride him down a different kind of aisle.

The memories are especially strong whenever I'm visiting friends in the Midwest, confronted by Bible Belt billboards:

"Knock, and Jesus will answer!" *Well, I did email several times to see if he wanted to get closure over coffee, but spake unto me, he did not.*

Nothing in spam, either.

Do you ever wonder about what might have been? Write a note to your one that got away.

"The heart wants what the heart wants, or else it does not care."

EMILY DICKINSON

FOREVER IN A DAY

PJ Bodnar

D ear Kristen,

After all these years, I doubt you even remember me, but there isn't a week that goes by that I don't think about you and that amazing day we shared in the California sun.

Your aunt and uncle told me you'd be coming into the winery where I worked that day. They didn't describe you. But the moment you and your friends walked in and our gaze locked, I could feel the energy between us. Your eyes were the same beautiful blue of the California sky that warmed the grapes on the vineyard's hills. And your smile lit up the room.

Your friends instantly noted our connection and the whispers and giggles began as they pushed you toward the wine bar. It took all the control I could muster not to spill the wine because I was so distracted by you.

We walked together as I gave the grand tour of the winery. And when your hand brushed mine, an electric spark shot through me. We were fighting the magnetic pull of the universe pushing us together. I know you felt it as acutely as I did. There was no way I wanted the moment to end, so I made up stories about the winery until my imagination ran out.

After the tour, your friends magically vanished into the vineyard, and it was just the two of us. But it had been just the two of us since the moment you walked in. How could this be the end?

I asked if we could see each other again.

You blushed, smiled, and said, "Yes."

We met at the trail that ran up the Santa Barbara foothills and overlooked the harbor and Pacific Ocean.

This day would end up being one I think about all the time.

It was so easy. You walked ahead for most of the narrow trail. Our conversations flowed, and when we reached the summit, we sat on a boulder and took in the view. Our bodies knew what we wanted, but we were afraid of what might happen. We didn't have to talk, and in the quiet, the tension pinged between us. So much was said but not a word was spoken.

Later we met for dinner at a little Italian restaurant and then walked to the Santa Barbara Pier with our ice cream desserts and sat on a bench.

That first kiss still lingers in my body.

The charge ran up my spine so intensely, and we both pulled away. At first I thought I had overstepped, but the look in your eyes said something very different. Then you uttered the word I hear over and over in my mind, "Wow."

The second kiss lasted an eternity and everyone on the pier disappeared. There was only us; everything else faded away. I don't know how long we sat there locked together on that bench. Our bodies didn't want to let go, couldn't let go of each other, and our souls didn't want to either.

As we walked back to your car, our hands held onto the moment. The last kiss had the passion of people who have been together for ages. Then you got into your car, and I watched your tail lights dim as you drove up State Street.

We never spoke again.

All my calls went unanswered.

Your aunt told me six months later that you had married someone, and had moved to be closer to his family.

I have never doubted that you felt the same energy between us. You can't fake that intensity, and I have never regretted meeting you. We shared a perfect moment that most people will never experience. It wasn't tarnished by normal life. Magic is best when you don't see what is behind the curtain.

There is little chance you will ever read this or maybe even know it's you I'm talking to.

I have worn a mask since that day. One I don't want to admit. The truth is, I compare all my other relationships to this one moment in time with you—a standard even you may not be able to meet now. One I doubt I could either. One I have been searching for and never found.

Sometimes I worry that I gave up too easily and settled for less, but maybe this ideal standard was only achievable for a day.

That one amazing day on California's central coast is ours forever. People talk about love at first sight, and I believe *that* is what we experienced that day, *even if only for a day.* And although we never saw each other again, we still share that precious gift.

Yours . . . forever in a day,

PJ

Do you believe in love at first sight? Why or why not? Has it ever happened to you?

Find words with four+ letters containing an "O"

THERE'S ONE LOVEY-DOVEY WORD THAT HAS ALL 7 LETTERS: _ _ _ _ _ _ _

Hint: 72 words total

"All romance is grounded
in friendship."

HENRY DAVID THOREAU

LAUGHTER IS OUR LOVE LANGUAGE

Lisa A. Mahoney

Very early in our marriage, my husband and I had a humdinger of a fight. Something stupid. Petty. A long one. Our bedroom stayed empty as we each, unbeknownst to the other, skulked off to sleep in different parts of the ten-room house we shared with his family. Days later, passing me in the hall, he said, "You know we can't ever get divorced—it will prove your mother right."

We laughed. And that became our peace treaty. Our fights end with laughter. Always.

The other day we were arguing about the dual settings on our air fryer. He frantically pushed buttons, arms flailing around like an octopus. I raised my voice, reaching around him to unpress and press them differently to demonstrate how the "match" feature worked. Exasperated, I yelled, "I don't understand," from one of our favorite rom-coms, *The Proposal*.

Without skipping a beat, he replied, "Why are you naked?"—Sandra Bullock's zinger in the chaotic scene.

And I came back with my best Ryan Reynolds yell, "Why are you wet?"

We forgot our tiff and cracked up.

These lines from *The Proposal* may seem odd, silly, even slightly inappropriate, but to us, they're our love language.

Our shared appreciation for random movie lines, or more frequently, obscure Geico and Progressive insurance commercials, is our "I love you."

Don't get me wrong—we say those three words, but they're not in our daily lexicon. Maybe that's because the words "I love you" were either nonexistent or transactional for both of us growing up. My husband's parents divorced acrimoniously when he was a teen, and while he remembers some expressions of love from his absentee father, his mother didn't utter the words until her actual dying days. Conversely, I heard the declaration from my parents often, but there was always a catch, a price, a quid pro quo.

So we didn't become the lovey-dovey couple.

In fact, our daughter once commented, "I've never seen you and Dad hold hands." Not even a little offended by this, I laughed.

But if you asked my daughter if she saw us laugh together, she'd say, "Every day." We're not into PDA (public displays of affection). We're not mushy in love.

It's been this way since we met.

An early example is when I started my first professional job out of college. We were newly married and broke. My birthday was approaching, so I asked my husband if instead of him buying me a gift I could go buy myself some professional clothes to fit my new role. I was not apt to frivolously spend on myself, so this was perfect. The day of my birthday came and I donned one of my new power suits, feeling pretty hip. However, it was pouring outside so I put on my raincoat—a bright yellow rain slicker like a toddler might wear. Feeling a little out-of-sync fashion-wise, I meekly asked my husband if I looked okay. He said yes so I went to work. That night, when I arrived home, he handed me a bag from a very expensive store (one I knew but had only window-shopped due to its extravagance). I got upset and said, "You were NOT supposed to buy me any gifts. I just spent way too much money on myself."

He replied, "It's not exactly a birthday gift. It's an apology."

Not grasping what he could possibly have done to warrant a mea culpa, I said, "For what?"

"For lying to you this morning. When you asked if you looked good, I said yes. But you really didn't."

The bag held a professional raincoat.

These "I love you"s have peppered our thirty-eight years together.

By many accounts, my husband and I are opposites. I'm books. He's sports. I'm the tortoise. He's the hare. I'm cautious and uptight. He's hasty and laid-back. I'm a creative thinker. He's methodical. I'm organized and he's, well . . . not. He tells people he married me for my filing skills. From the days of us first dating, people have commented on our very different dispositions.

Not too long ago at an event, I overheard a friend and my sister-in-law talking about me and my husband and our longevity as a couple.

My friend said, "In some ways I can't believe they're still together."

My sister-in-law said, "Oh, that's easy to believe. Many couples stay together. What I can't believe is that they still make each other laugh every single day."

I smiled. Our marriage is not a full-on mushy display of "I love you" and hand-holding and fawning but in the wise words of Shrek, "That'll do, donkey. That'll do."

WAITING FOR YOU

Mark Mathias

In mid-June of 1982, with no particular destination in mind, I drove away from the San Francisco Bay Area for a two-week road trip. Youthful curiosity and a love of nature led me to a remote camping spot high in the mountains of northern New Mexico.

That first night, sitting next to a cozy fire and staring up at the carpet of stars above me, I *pleaded* to the cosmos—to God—for confirmation that I was on the right path in my life. My prayer, my declaration to the universe, was that I'd done all the right things and was now experienced and mature enough—at the age of twenty-six—to be worthy of Great Love.

I waited.

Except for the crackle of the fire, there was silence, dead calm.

Then tears.

After a moment, while continuing to look into the night sky, a wordless, empathetic response came through: *I hear you . . . I understand . . . It's going to be okay . . .*

Once back home from the road trip, I returned to my life as the drummer for a popular Bay Area band, a time in my life when intimate relationships came and went easily.

I had my favorites—Linda Ronstadt/Ali MacGraw look-alikes—but now, after my fireside God chat in New Mexico, I was prepared to accept that she—The One—might not fit the mold.

I put that fireside moment into a song:

Sometimes when I think about
The way my life is turning out
I wonder if I'll die a lonely man.
Maybe that's the price I pay
For mistakes I've made along the way
But if you think you have a better plan
I'm waiting for you . . .

Whoever and wherever she might be, I'd be right here: experienced enough to know that the buzz-glow thing at the front end of new relationships eventually wears off, mature enough to know that the stress of maintaining first-date facades and projections eventually becomes so untenable that who we *truly* are begins to bleed through.

God knows that I've learned a lot
And now I know what love is not
And I can't give what isn't mine to give
Maybe you can help me find
The kind of love I have in mind
The kind that has sustained me as I've lived
Waiting for you

A few months later I came home from a gig at 1:30 a.m. and recorded in a journal that I think I've finally met her: Eilene—slender, blonde, dark eyes; a singer who had just arrived from New York to begin a new life in northern California. She loved the band, admired my playing, my healthy lifestyle, and my love of nature.

Twenty hours later, at my next gig, I met Lisa: pudgy, brunette, a smoker; a spirited Bette Midler doppelganger, just arrived from Chicago to begin a new life in northern California. I enjoyed talking to her so much that when she asked me to sign a copy of the band's new record, I set aside my peeled orange and wrote: *To Lisa, Welcome to California! You are loved . . . Mark.*

Eilene became my girlfriend. We lasted a little over a year—a record for me—by which time she had borrowed and wrecked my car, never paying for repairs; borrowed my credit card to buy furniture for her new apartment, never paying me back . . . and then the band broke up.

Lisa, meanwhile, had become my *best* friend. We shared New Age spirituality, music, wine, animated conversations about life's meaning and the continuing search for our respective true loves.

Our clothes came off for others, but not for each other; not for seven years, anyway. The night before she left to work production on a rock star's world tour, our clothes *did* come off for each other, and our relationship instantly went from BFF to WTF.

She returned from that tour a year later, engaged to a redneck tour bus driver from Tennessee. By the time she'd moved *there*, married him and had a son, I was living with my latest girlfriend, soon to be the mother of our daughter.

My dysfunctional marriage lasted longer than both of Lisa's—sixteen years—by which time she had launched her son and moved back to the Bay Area, twelve miles from my newly-acquired, unfurnished bachelor cottage, where I was now singing *Waiting for You* to myself almost daily; in the soundtrack of my life, it had become the main theme.

Too bad I wasn't perceptive enough to realize I'd written that song about someone who was already in my life, and had been, for more than twenty years.

One day, Lisa announced that she'd saved every email we'd exchanged during the years of our respective dysfunctional married lives. On a whim, we printed the emails. Two reams later, we began an ongoing game of randomly pulling sheets from the stack and reading them aloud to one another, and later publishing those emails in a book with names changed to protect the not-so-innocent.

The last of those emails ends with the day in September of 2010 that I moved into my bachelor cottage, still convinced I've yet to meet The One and having privately declared that, from here on out, God will captain my love boat; my role will be to *stay* on the boat, regardless of destination, and say *yes* to the adventure.

When that boat sailed for southern New Mexico in the spring of 2018, Lisa was already on it. Looking back now, I see that she'd been on it this whole time, waiting for *me*, since the day I signed her record in October of 1982.

These days, when sitting around crackling fires in the backyard of our Pueblo-style home, Lisa and I look up at the stars, feeling grateful that the long wait is not only over, it was worth it.

"If you love somebody, let them go,
for if they return, they were always
yours. If they don't,
they never were."

KAHLIL GIBRAN

HEART LINE

Lisa Lucca

The fortune teller took my left hand and studied my palm. "You will have a great love," she said, tracing the line beneath my fingers. "You may already know him."

My repeatedly broken heart fluttered.

"You'll be older." She nodded, satisfied. "But finally happy."

"How *much* older?" I asked.

"Around fifty." She released my hand. *Fifty!?* At thirty-five, that felt utterly ancient.

"Great. I'll probably end up in the desert with my friend, Mark . . . when we're old," I declared. Odd, since we hadn't spoken in years. Mark was a drummer I met when I landed in San Francisco at twenty-one. We became dear friends and never dated—unless you count that one night we slept together before I left to help produce a world tour with Janet Jackson. The morning after, I wrote in my journal that I didn't have to worry if he called because I'd be gone for a year. *Someday we'll end up together in New Mexico,* I scrawled—a curious intuition. I returned a year later, engaged to a roadie. Mark had moved in with his girlfriend.

My quest for true love had been the center of my desires all my life. "Lisa has daddy issues," some would say, and of course they would be right. Dad was a selfish, charismatic genius whose love I spent decades chasing. I pursued boys, then men, to soothe the ache in my heart. Until I collided with a good ole boy from Tennessee while out on the road. His charm and swagger were enough for me to marry him but not to keep me from leaving the suffocating marriage before our fifth anniversary with our three-year-old son in tow. I had morphed into the wife he wanted from the woman I was—a witchy bohemian who believed in things like palm readers. By hiding my tarot cards and crystals, I thought I could let go of that part of me. But, no.

The thing about true love is that truth is at the heart of it. It makes you want to be your most authentic self. I wasn't.

Mark once called me out of the blue while I was still married. "I've been thinking about becoming a studio drummer in Nashville," he said, while I fed my son Zac in his high chair. "What do you think?" His voice was a cool breeze blowing fresh air into my stale life. *Boy, I miss him.* We had bounced every career and romantic idea off one another for years, putting our intentions on paper with a crystal in an ashtray.

"Yeah! Great idea." We chatted about music, my domesticated life, his baby daughter and recent shotgun wedding. My thoughts drifted to seeing him again, his nimble body playing drums, kissing his chiseled face . . . until my son got fussy, bringing me back to reality.

"It's so good to hear your voice, Lis. Call you soon."

A few years passed before I heard from Mark again. It was after my discontentment led to divorce. After I moved back to Chicago. After the palm reading that revived thoughts of ending up together in the desert.

We began emailing. During a visit to California, I called to invite him and his wife to a dinner party. All the guests canceled for one reason or another. He arrived alone. We cooked, we danced, we laughed—both realizing we wanted what we couldn't have . . . this magical love that would not be still.

When I got home, an email arrived: "We can't talk for a while. It's too hard." I cried buckets and went back on Match.com, where I met someone new, then another, but none of them was Mark.

After a year, Mark's emails resumed. We poured our hearts out about love, parenting, God, purpose, and expectations that hadn't been realized well into our forties. The next time I was in town, we met for drinks and walked in the moonlight. "You feel like home to me," he whispered with a gentle kiss before sending me back to single motherhood, my work, and Match.com, where I met Dave. He reminded me of Mark in the way Pergo flooring can pass for Brazilian cherry hardwood. In the right light, with enough wine, it looks like the real thing. A year after we met, I married him.

"I was going to send you guys a case of wine, but what I really want is to have him whacked," Mark wrote.

"We like red," I replied. The wine never arrived, and our emails stopped.

Not long after the wedding, another psychic said, "Your twin flame is a sage," her eyes sparkling. "Oh, that's probably my friend, Mark," I replied matter-of-factly, then asked why my new marriage had already grown contentious. "Focus on you," she instructed, not wanting to say we were doomed. It wasn't long before my second marriage buckled under the weight of mediocrity, and we divorced, too.

On a business trip to Sacramento that autumn, I drove through the wine country to meet Mark at the Napa library. The lush beauty of California called me home to who I was before husbands and motherhood.

"I'm moving back," I said softly, kissing his cheek to greet him. "When Zac heads to college."

"Hurry up," he said, beaming.

Mark never told me he would leave his unhappy marriage for us. I never asked him to. We just knew if I was there and he was free, we would be together.

I turned fifty in my charming cottage by the San Francisco Bay, celebrating with friends and Mark, who was, by then, unfettered and in his own place. It took time to find a rhythm to our romance. We lived apart for several years, making our way back to ourselves; we spent our weekends and trips to Italy exploring our love and each other. Nearly three decades after I wrote my premonition, Mark and I moved into an enchanted home in New Mexico together. But not before I broke my left hand, deepening the heart line that had known our destiny all along. It was just waiting for us to catch up.

"Real love and truth are stronger than an evil or misfortune."

CHARLES DICKENS

THE WORDS HE SAYS

Audrey Wick

He told me my scars were beautiful, which is what a husband is supposed to say to a wife. Still, I was grateful for someone telling me such words because I wasn't finding beauty in how I looked.

Brian, though, saw my scars long before I did. Lying in the hospital bed after my emergency brain surgery for a ruptured aneurysm at age thirty-nine, I wouldn't encounter a mirror until week two of my ICU stay. But he saw me from day one, forming memories and images from that time that I don't have. In that way, he had a head start in reacting to my scars, which were not simply contained to my head.

Brain surgery, after all, is complicated.

Aside from a PICC line in my arm, scars were forming across the crescent-shaped shaved spot and staple incisions on the top of my scalp, at the tubing that now ran internally from my brain to my abdomen, with stitch points behind my ear and across my belly, and in a series of triple notches in my upper right leg as well. All these entry points were for procedures that collectively saved my life.

Some people say scars are a sign of strength, badges of honor to be worn with pride. All I knew was that I was nowhere near that viewpoint early in my recovery.

So after hospital discharge, long sleeves hid my arms bruised from prods and pricks. Cloth headbands and strategically parted hair in a new direction hid my scalp incision wounds. Button-only tops and loose pants allowed my lower body scars to breathe but not be seen.

As I recovered in the weeks and months post-surgery, I tried to make peace with my body. But the smallest of tasks—trying to brush my hair or finally pulling a top over my head—were reminders of the brain aneurysm that, while now treated, would be something I would never actually divest.

That's what no one ever told me: aneurysms stay with a person. And when the brain bleeds, it also short-circuits everything. While I expected head-related pain, it was the reverberating aches, weaknesses, and soreness in different parts of my body that made recovery a long road. Visual reminders, too, made moving forward difficult.

So I couldn't help asking: would my body ever be my own again?

And in the absence of my being able to answer that, Brian did.

Yes.

He never acted as if I were broken. Whispered words of encouragement when I needed them the most coupled with affectionate gestures helped me find a path forward. He never flinched when I removed my headbands or if I exposed my scars at home. He would instead offer a warm touch, a close kiss, or trace his finger near the wounds soundlessly, as if they held magic.

Watching him helped me guide my own reactions. For in quiet moments, I too would privately trace my scars, trying to absorb strength from their shapes.

With time, I was able to eventually do that. Time helped me heal, but Brian did too. His guidance was my North Star. True love is like that, a beacon to guide the other person in the relationship through the most trying of times.

Brian still tells me my scars are beautiful, and now when he does, I meet him at that place—and believe him.

LOVE DURING COVID LOCKDOWN

Denise Hoth

"That was Camp Bow Wow," I said to Kristy as I hung up the phone. It was early March—2020. "They're shutting down the kennel because of Covid."

My two-year-old mixed-breed rescue dog, Ruby, was boarded near my home in the Chicago suburbs while I was visiting Kristy, who lived in Milwaukee. Ruby was my best friend, wing girl, and canine love of my life. Kristy was my smart, beautiful, fun-loving new girlfriend, whom I had met online six weeks earlier. Human love of my life? TBD.

Kristy and I had been seeing each other on weekends, alternating between homes, getting to know one another when the Covid lockdown hit. It was still super early in the relationship, and while we seemed to have a lot in common, she was different from anyone I had dated before. And I liked that. Sweet and soft-spoken, she could make me laugh at the drop of a hat. She had already met my friends and fit in; I had been introduced to her identical twin sister and we hit it off. It appeared this girl was a keeper. Although she did have a cat.

"Why don't you and Cecil stay with Ruby and me until things open up again? Lockdown will be 'two weeks to flatten the curve.' It could be fun," I offered.

Now, I know what you're thinking: cue the U-Haul commercial with the cute lesbians who move in together after their second date. But that's not me. The last time I lived with a partner it took us eight years to cohabitate, and that relationship had ended eight years prior. I was a solo act, just me and my dog, and here I had just invited this stunning woman and her gorgeous cat to come stay with us. Was I crazy? In the moment, unsure of where the world was headed, it felt like the right thing to do. We didn't know if the border between our states would close, had little information about the fast-moving, highly-contagious disease killing people across the world, plus this new romance was just getting underway. Kristy agreed—we would hunker down together. We packed her and the cat (including the litter box, accessories, and cat tree . . . really, cats need trees?) into my SUV, then headed south. Next stop: my house, Chicago.

Neither Ruby nor Cecil had ever seen the other's species before. There were frantic chases and a few standoffs, but within a few days they figured out the pecking order, mostly because Cecil was able to outsmart Ruby at every turn and they became friends.

Kristy and I? We had no trouble settling into daily life. We both worked from home pre-lockdown; she's an insurance claims adjuster and I'm in the surgical equipment industry, so we were fortunate enough to continue our full-time jobs during quarantine. I gave Kristy my kitchen table to set up her office. From my work station in the lower level of my two-bedroom rowhouse, I could hear her conduct business. She knew her stuff and skillfully calmed clients through crises. Witnessing her in action, sharing her vast knowledge of insurance, and seeing her genuine concern for her clients made her even more attractive. Kristy's kindness and intelligence were so sexy.

In the evenings and on weekends, we played. I pulled out my old Guitar Hero video game and she kicked my ass. We watched endless YouTube music videos (by the end of lockdown I knew every word to every song in *Hamilton*). Meeting up with *our* friends for Zoom happy hours became a regular evening activity. (Wait, did I just say "our" friends? Yep, they were "our" friends by then.) We talked—a lot. Being together twenty-four-seven so early in our relationship gave us a crash course in each other's lives. Life was good, and I was falling. Gulp.

A few weeks in I set up an in-home pub crawl, creating different drinks and themes in each room. A wine bar at the kitchen island, an Irish pub at the breakfast bar, and even a "swim-up" martini bar in the master bath, which we didn't make it to after the bourbon tasting in the living room. With the real bars closed, it was the closest we had to going on a date. A bit corny, but we had fun!

Truth is, we had missed out on some early dating rituals by sheltering in place together. Going out for the evening was replaced by dishwasher-loading discussions and breaking up spats between our fur babies. The pandemic shaped our budding romantic relationship in a unique and tender way that I'd not previously experienced. I mean, even the move-right-in U-Haul lesbians could leave the house, right?

As the stay-at-home order began to lift, it became clear to us that a decision had to be made. Should Kristy and Cecil go home?

It was tempting to make our living arrangement permanent, but it was too soon. Kristy had ended a ten-year relationship the previous autumn and was re-establishing herself in Milwaukee. My business was in the middle of a few significant changes, and I didn't want to leave my elderly mother who lived nearby. Neither of us could pick up our life and relocate. But that was okay. By now, we knew we were in love and that was enough.

Two months after the "two-week lockdown to flatten the curve" had begun, I drove Kristy and Cecil back to Wisconsin (cat tree included). The next morning, as I pulled my empty SUV away from her place, I felt a hollow ache in my stomach. Nevertheless I smiled, because my heart knew that one day I'd be navigating a packed U-Haul full of Kristy's and

LOVE❤NOTES!

Cecil's belongings and we'd be headed into a life together—and a place we would call *our* home.

COOKING WITHOUT RECIPES

Rebecca Thatcher Murcia

The saying goes that the way to a man's heart is through his stomach. I am not a man, though I do have one very persistent chin hair. The aphorism was true in my case. Shortly after Saúl's beautiful eyes and bright smile caught my attention at a party in Brownsville, Texas, where he was volunteering with the Mennonite church and I was working at the local newspaper, he showed up at my home with bacon and Parmesan cheese and whipped up an amazing plate of tasty pasta. I later learned that it was called carbonara, but in any case, it was delicious, and it was love at first bite.

We married a year later, and he continued to surprise me with spontaneously made dishes that were rich and spicy and often redolent with the flavors of garlic and cilantro. Saúl had been trained as a chef in his native Colombia and he was skilled with a knife, often cutting fruit and vegetables into boats and animals. Later, he would delight our children by carving a puercoespín (porcupine) out of a mango.

I had never been a very dedicated cook but have always been a dedicated eater. I love to eat and would probably weigh three hundred pounds if I weren't also a complete soccer addict. I could cook, but it involved the laborious process of finding a good recipe in the *Joy of Cooking* I inherited from my mother, shopping for the ingredients, and then carefully following the step-by-step instructions.

I was happily freeloading off Saúl's fantastic kitchen work when one day I came home and there was a note: "Vengo como a las siete." Completely misunderstanding *como* as the first-person present tense of comer, I thought he meant, "I need to eat at seven," instead of, "I'll be home at about seven." I began frantically scavenging, panicking about what to make for my husband, who for some reason needed to eat at precisely seven. I searched the refrigerator for cilantro and then started frying garlic and onions, the way Saúl started most of his culinary creations. When he walked in the door, I rushed to apologize for not having the food ready at seven. He laughed and explained my grammar confusion.

Misunderstandings about Spanish homophones notwithstanding, we forged ahead to Austin, where we both had jobs and our sons were born. When the Mennonites offered him a whole $40,000 a year to be director of international programs, we moved to Pennsylvania.

He never stopped being our family chef, although he liked to cook alone. A lifelong soccer player, he would raise an imaginary red card in the air when you tried to help him and ask to be left in peace—that is, until he no longer could stand, much less cook alone or wield a knife with his customary ease. He got a terrible case of bone cancer.

Cooking became social. In the last few months of his life, we were surrounded by friends and family. My mother. His sister. Our church community. We would follow his cooking instructions, and I would secretly take notes. Saúl was all about living that last spring to the fullest. I didn't want to draw attention to his terminal diagnosis, and I would one day need to remember these recipes.

Then when our sons were eight and nine, he succumbed, leaving us heartbroken. Suddenly I had lost my children's father, my companion, a beloved man, and our chef.

So how was I supposed to go into the kitchen every day? How was I to touch that third rail of my grief, handling the same pots and pans and knives that Saúl had wielded with such skill? How?!

Awful.

And these boys needed to eat every bloody day!

But I did it. Unlike Saúl, I relied on recipes. And I remembered what Saúl said when we were saving to buy a house in Austin: "We'll have rice and beans on Monday, and beans and rice on Tuesday." I even extended those beans for tacos, burgers, and enchiladas.

I kept at it, and eventually I became a better cook, less dependent on written instructions. To this day, nineteen years later, Saúl's wise counsel—*to be patient when frying onions and to keep tasting to see if the spices are right*—is always on my mind.

Oh. And never forget the cilantro.

WAITING IN THE WINDOW'S WINGS WITH A WARM WAVE

Scott Thomas Outlar

It feels exciting, even engaging,
to be alive

but to love is bliss
and to be loved is electric

so if a smile is contagious

then our synchronized dance
might just cause
   a hypnotic pandemic

two-step

    tango

heal-all tea

    portents of potent potions

I had more than faith

that you were always near

"Grow old along with me! The best is yet to be, the last of life, for which the first was made."

ROBERT BROWNING

HEARTS THAT SING TWICE

Bella Ruth Bader and Philip J. Palladino

As a sliver of light crept under the window shade, Bella peered at sleepy Phil.

"Good morning, my love," Bella cheerfully whispered.

Phil perked up with a big smile. "Good morning to you, my love, Bella." He nuzzled into her curly hair. "Let's make minestrone soup today."

"First, we'll walk at eight," Bella said, rolling over. "I'll do my stretches while you have your coffee."

They made the bed in the predawn darkness, then hugged again, lingering in the embrace, grateful for this quiet morning and the path that had led them, in their eighties, to this moment.

*

Six years ago, I was a widower alone and on vacation in Mexico. That Monday, I toured the scenic village of Dolores Hidalgo, talking mostly to the bus driver, since he and I were the only non-partnered people in the group. Seeing couples together heightened my yearning for a similar relationship. I wondered if I could be lucky a second time.

After I returned to my Airbnb and took a nap, I wandered the streets of San Miguel de Allende as dusk fell, searching for something sweet to soothe my heart. As fate would have it, the aroma from the Panio Bakery lured me into its quaint little cafe. As soon as I spotted the cakes, my loneliness dissipated. I found a cozy spot and sat down at a white bistro table, with a rich, chocolate, cream-filled cake and a cup of dark coffee, feeling like a king.

An attractive woman with white curly hair approached the cashier in search of the cafe's Wi-Fi password. She turned to me as I dove into the chocolate and asked if I knew the code. She figured it out herself, made the connection, and her bright eyes fixed on me as she inquired with a broad smile, "Are you alone?" That woman was Bella Ruth Bader.

*

That man was Phil Palladino. He had warm brown eyes and strong large hands. His spontaneous smile touched me when he offered to join me at my table. Our conversation effortlessly flowed from one subject to the next. It turned out that we lived relatively close to each other; we were both in the mental health field; we had common friends; we had both lost our loving spouses recently; we enjoyed travel and hiking; we each had children and grandchildren. Most of all, we found the other to be a very good listener, and we didn't want our conversation to end.

When the cafe closed and it was chilly outside, what a surprise it was to have Phil accompany me back to Casa Calderoni. Our hands snuggled warmly in Phil's hoodie pocket while we continued sharing where we came from, and whom we've become.

I've always sought adventure. By age seven, I rode city buses and trains unaccompanied in the Bronx and Brooklyn. It didn't surprise my loved ones that I would explore Japan for five weeks only one year after my loving husband suddenly died. Nor were they alarmed that I would travel to San Miguel de Allende alone in 2018 for the month of February. There, I had been meeting new people, attending classical and jazz concerts and art and museum openings. Still, somewhere deep in my heart, I longed for love again. I knew that I needed to be patient while enjoying my life without a partner. I imagined that if I were to be lucky a second time, love would find me.

When we arrived at the casa, I rang the doorbell. It was time for Phil to leave, but neither of us wanted the night to end. I wondered when we would meet again. Although we had traded email addresses, we had not made another plan before we said goodbye. My heart fluttered. Could I be falling in love again?

*

With visions of Bella dancing in my head, I floated over the cobblestones to my Airbnb, through the vibrant San Felipe Neri Plaza with my heart dancing. Our parting had been abrupt when our hands became disentangled too quickly, and Bella disappeared through the entrance of the casa. It's not the end, I thought. Skip the writing workshop tomorrow. Got to see Bella.

*

I was exhilarated when Phil called to tell me that he would rather be with me than go to his seminar. We spent that warm, sunny day walking to Fabrica la Aurora. We both loved the turn-of-the-century textile mill that had been restored into art galleries and artists' studios. As we traded our observations and thoughts about the art, a strong bond began to form. That night, back in my casa, sitting with my new friends around the glowing fireplace, I was excited to tell them that I was in love.

*

This lonely man's heart once again started to sing. On Valentine's Day, I surprised Bella with a small bouquet of wildflowers, before I left on a scheduled eight-hour bus trip to my writing retreat in Tepoztlán. I hated to be tugged away from Bella. Email became our loveline for the next couple of weeks. My new love for Bella overflowed into almost every conversation with my writing peers, even as I discussed my memoir that included my devotion for my late wife. Soon, I returned to upstate New York, a mere two-hour drive to Bella's home.

*

Only six years later, we have created our own book of memories with family and friends. We've kept our separate houses and lives in our hometowns, but often wonder about living together full-time. Perhaps this fifty-fifty living arrangement is the key to our successful relationship?

We hold hands as we walk up a country road in the early morning. The fall landscape is bright and we greet carpenters restoring an old house on our way. We hear the birdsong, experience the wind, and peer into the forest in search of new sights. After a mile and a half, we return to share a breakfast of jointly prepared warm oatmeal garnished with fruit and nuts; arrange to see the play *Lunar Eclipse* at Shakespeare and Company; discuss a future Amtrak trip to Montreal; and we make the minestrone.

Our rich harvest soup has distinct colors, tastes, and textures: purple onions, orange carrots, stranded celery, spongy spinach, red kidney beans, white garbanzos, noodles, and Italian spices. Absolutely delicious and warming on a cool autumn night.

IMAGINE THE LOVE NOTES THAT PASSED BETWEEN THESE FAMOUS COUPLES!

ACROSS

1. Samson's girl
3. He gave up a rib for his smoking hot chick
7. He couldn't handle his feelings for Juliet

DOWN

2. Mark Anthony totally dug this woman
4. Beyonce's husband
5. Johnny's best gal

RESETTING THE BAR

Katie McCollow

When my mother, Punkin, was in second grade, her father took off, leaving his wife and five children to fend for themselves. The youngest two—my mom and her little brother—were sent to live with the nuns for a few years while my grandmother figured out how to support her family without a husband. My dad, John, once described his own father to me as "the meanest SOB I've ever met," a man physically and emotionally abusive to his wife and kids.

John and Punkin met at a golf tournament in northern Minnesota in the summer of 1955. Dad, an already established writer at the *Reader's Digest,* was playing in it, and my mother, a twenty-year-old nursing student, was there as the guest of mutual friends. At first, her casual clamdiggers and bucket hat caused Dad to mistake her for a caddie, which Mom found hilarious. Later that same evening, she wrapped herself in delicious blue satin and sashayed into the club's dining room, where he took one look at her and told his friends he was going to marry her.

The clamdiggers were more on-brand for her than the satin. Casual and carefree is my mother's vibe—she rarely wears jewelry, even though she has a pirate's booty of sparkly baubles gifted to her by her adoring spouse. Dad traveled a lot, and he always returned with a trinket for her, like the star-sapphire ring flanked with diamonds he presented her with "because you are the star of our family."

Mom returned his doting, happily fulfilling the role of homemaker, but also serving as his most trusted editor. He'd call her into his office and read to her whatever story he was working on, listening respectfully to her feedback and bouncing ideas off of her.

They were always affectionate, regularly holding hands and making eyes at each other, even with their noisy brood of nine children underfoot.

"I don't need that stuff while you're around," I once overheard my octogenarian father chortle to my mother in response to a Cialis commercial. She hooted. He always made her laugh.

They were codependent in the best way.

"We have diabetes," Mom announced one day, about twenty years ago. "We? What?" we asked. "The doctor says your father has diabetes, and we're going to control it through diet," she said, not the slightest speck of doubt in her voice or resolution. Their united front kicked *their* diabetes to the curb in short order.

In 2018, at the age of ninety, my dad fell and broke his neck. He shouldn't have survived the fall or the subsequent surgery, but he did because Mom expected him to. She didn't beg him to hang on or plead to the universe—she simply prayed and manifested his recovery.

Every day, as soon as she'd dressed and finished her coffee, off to the rehab facility she went to read him the paper, hold his useless hands, and set the tone in no uncertain terms—*get better, get out of bed, and get your ass back home.*

And he did. After three months of Herculean effort, he was strong enough to leave. The physical therapists were astounded, but his children weren't—he wasn't about to let his girl down. Over the next two years, he even regained his ability to walk and type a bit again.

One day when he was still in rehab, my mother brought him fixings for a root beer float. "He can't have that," his nurse said.

"It's our sixty-second anniversary." Mom smiled and proceeded to spoon-feed him his favorite treat, latent diabetes and patient protocols be damned.

In early 2020, Mom developed a yellowish tinge, so she had a blood draw. *A rare blood cancer*, they told her—*Oh, also you have Covid. We're locking you here for two weeks, and no one can visit.* My dad cried.

He needn't have worried. Two weeks later Mom was home, the Covid hardly affecting her. The bad news was, she'd been given four to eighteen months to live because of the blood thing. I write it as casually as my mother (doing basically fine, five years later) considers it.

Dad's body began its final descent in mid-2020. His doctor suggested hospice, but Mom insisted it was the lockdown that had made him sedentary and he just needed to get stronger. Back into rehab he went, her stubborn refusal to acknowledge there's no cure for being ninety-three endearing and frustrating in equal measure.

The therapists explained no exercises would help Dad this time and sent him home. In his final days, he mostly slept, but his eyes sometimes fluttered open and Mom would take his hand and say, "I'm here, Johnny," and he'd smile and close them again. He transitioned peacefully, surrounded by his large and loving family.

Now, seeing pictures of my elderly dad near the end of his life, Mom is shocked.

"He never looked old to me," she says. "He always looked like the dashing young man I married."

Mom has stumped her doctors—they've never had a patient with her condition, at her age, do so well. She's happy to still be here, but I also know when her time comes, she'll look forward to making another grand entrance that will knock Johnny's socks off. They'll be holding hands and flirting with each other, as they wait for the giant crowd their sixty-four years of love together produced to join them.

HIM AND JIM

Ellen O'Neill

I'm eighty-five years old, a bit tired, gray, and wrinkled. My walking and balance are compromised. My hearing is failing. My vision is impaired. Physically and emotionally there is much in life that is unpleasant. I try to keep up with the news and stay as caring, active, and alert as my body, mind, and spirit allow. I am learning to live with the vast losses that accompany aging. Like most old folks, I spend time reminiscing. I tally what I have accomplished and regret what I have not, and I go on.

This morning, my memories returned to the 1970s. I was in my thirties, trim, firm, and pretty. My twenties were spent in a marriage to an abusive husband to whom I offered abject obedience in whatever way he commanded and demanded, which had made me terribly unhappy. Back then, no Catholic, Italian-American girl with four children would leave her husband. I did. I divorced my husband!

Newly single, I envisioned myself as liberated, never to marry again. My intent was to grow from a girl to a woman. Like Helen Reddy sang, I would be strong, smart, and invincible, or at least that was the plan.

Braless and brave, I helped lead the longest teachers' strike in New York State's history to a very successful outcome. I marched against the

Vietnam War, rallied for civil rights, and indeed, I took my part in the women's movement.

The divorce was not easy. I was alone and judged harshly by family and friends. I cried all the time. After a while, I willed my sobs to cease. I decided it was time to *get out there*. Surprise, I discovered dating in the 1970s was nowhere near what it was like when I last dated back in the 1950s.

For example: Sex? I still believed *that* was reserved for marriage.

And marijuana? All I knew of pot had to do with cooking. I was a fish out of water swimming into new, sometimes dangerous, exciting seas. I only went out with any man for no more than two dates with no exceptions. I did not want to get involved.

Until I met *him* at White Pond. It was the summer of 1973. Wearing a blue seersucker fitted pantsuit, five-inch heels, and no underwear, I looked gorgeous.

So began the first fling of my life with a much younger man.

Why not? What the F$*K?

He took my hand and helped me into his canoe. He paddled to the middle of the pond. Me, him, the canoe, no one else. I remember it like this:

HIM: Close your eyes, listen.

ELLEN: I hear birds singing, the wind humming.

HIM: Open your eyes and observe one tree, only one.

ELLEN: I do.

HIM: Is it moving?

ELLEN: No.

HIM : Look again.

ELLEN: Yes! Yes! It's moving.

HIM: Now look, all around . . . further . . . deeper.

ELLEN: Oh, my! They're all moving.

HIM: Now, get undressed and slip into the water.

I blushed beet red, head to toe. Oh God, the water was cold. My inverted nipples popped out. The water sparkled, diamonds surrounded me, and fish nibbled at my tummy. All that was dry was wet. Music percolated the air. And for the first time in my life, I knew what making love was.

But it was what it was . . . a fling, a liaison, a short-lived romance. Still, it was wonderful.

Now it was time to get real.

I had been divorced for three years, and though I hate admitting it, I needed a steady guy in the house. I needed to be married. I had two boys entering puberty at a time when drugs and free love were de rigueur. I also had a seven-year-old son, a five-year-old daughter, and an ex-husband hell-bent on taking my children away from me. I had no money. I needed help. What the hell! What was the worst that could happen? I'd get divorced? Been there, done that.

So, I met Jim, and boy, was he handsome. Me? I was a bra burner and a liberal, but Jim, well, he was a straightlaced New York City cop. I was outgoing and Jim was quiet. I was a clutterer, and Jim was as neat as can be.

We both were coming out of hopeless marriages. We both had a first child who had died. He didn't paint or fix things; I didn't want to cook or clean. He worked nights. I worked days. This translated into a match made in heaven. When we married, my friends presented Jim with a purple heart, because who marries a woman with four children? Was this a cosmic joke? He dispelled all my stereotypes about cops. Well, almost all.

We, two very different people, stayed together and raised my four children, all successful college graduates who maintain meaningful positions in life. I am also gifted with six brilliant, beautiful grandchildren.

I'm Ellen, and at eighty-five years old, I'm still here. People see me as a crone. But this "old bag" is happy and still in love with Jim. Our love is deep, tender, and hopeful. I love that he makes me coffee and sings to me every morning. I love his ongoing unconditional support. I love everything we share. (Yes, even the fights and squabbles.) I love that we finish each other's sentences, and are always there for each other to fill in what the other forgets. I love that he respects me, that we will never part *and that I have no doubts this is true*.

Granted, life is short. I am not thinking of endings but of our future which, I believe, holds eternal love. This July, Jim and I celebrated a wonder-filled fifty years together.

If you could travel back in time and give your younger self one piece of advice about love, what would it be?

PEGGY SUE

Michael Owens

Like an owl observing the world, I sat at a college cafeteria table with my best friend and roommate beside me, passing judgment on the room of captive female beauties.

Peggy Sue was two tables away. She was oblivious to my arrow of romantic thoughts. She did not offer a casual smile or even look my way. I hadn't been lucky enough to talk to or "accidentally" bump into her at the college post office. In my heart I knew, once we met, she would have the qualities of honesty, trust, caring, and commitment I recognized in her kind face.

Outside, a misty rain among a stand of old pine trees had become a determined drizzle. The meal was finished and everyone began to drift to the open doors. Boys' dorms were to the left, women's to the right. Girls popped open umbrellas and dashed away. Others like me stood dumbfounded as the rain came down in sheets. Peggy Sue popped open her beige umbrella and I made my move.

"May I walk you to your dorm?" I stepped to her side.

Startled, she nodded in sympathetic agreement, and we stepped in unison into the heavy rain and onto the puddled path. At the stoop of her dorm doors, I asked if I might borrow the umbrella and return it when the rain stopped.

That is how I met my Peggy Sue.

We married four years later and a year after that, our twin boys were born two months premature. One doctor suggested an autopsy would be needed before one son would reach his second day of life. The other son was rushed to another hospital where better care was available. Miracle of miracles, neither child was blind nor deaf and each learned to walk on time. But I was fired from my job because my children's health care cost too much. I bounced from job to job and we moved from place to place. Peggy Sue stayed beside me with each step and every up and down, finding what work she could. I tried to make a living writing stories for print publications but the money was never enough. Still, Peggy Sue, ever the miracle worker, could stretch a single chicken to a full week of evening meals. We flipped a few houses and built a tiny nest egg. My father died at age fifty, so I was sure Peggy Sue would outlive me, as her mother had reached age one hundred. We found a good financial advisor and planned accordingly.

We loved each other and said so every day. Our agreement was to say "I love you the most" every time we parted. Love was a decision we made and a promise we kept.

With each anniversary, birthday, and Valentine's Day, I wrote a few lines of verse to celebrate our union. She slipped every love note I'd ever given her, along with the boys' little drawings, in unused wedding invitation envelopes and kept them in a cedar box gifted by her mother.

With time, the boys left the nest for college, finding their mates and settling states away. And then it was just the two of us. She cried every night for a year missing her sons so much. But we had climbed the ladder of life one rung at a time, and like our first rainy stroll in unison, we were a team and would this new chapter together—the medical drama of old age. Two knee replacements helped her mobility, but even with these replacement parts, walking was hard and she spent most of her time indoors. Still, this didn't stop us from finally traveling.

We went to London on a lark, spent time in Prague and Berlin, then went on some of those Viking cruises you see advertised. Peggy Sue even took her elderly mother on a Mississippi River cruise. We wore out our welcome overseas and began to travel in the States.

On one of our last winter trips while exploring Washington DC, we inadvertently lost each other at the crowded Dupont Circle subway entrance. Shivering, Peggy Sue waited for me in the cold until a kind, observant Metro guard realized we were searching for one another. He stayed with her until I arrived and took her to the hospital, where it was declared she had hypothermia.

Peggy Sue made exquisite quilts for the boys, their wives, and our grandchildren—hours captured in the years of pulling threads. On our last trip, we spent four months on the road to celebrate our fifty years of marriage. We covered half the country, but saved the rest for next year. We rushed from Philadelphia, where we attended an impending grandchild's baby shower, to New York to visit our other son's family, and then home to Houston, cutting the trip short because she was tired.

The next day, dressed in her flower blouse and white pants, she perched at her favorite stool at the kitchen counter. She smiled her sweet possum grin and pointed to the coffee pot.

"I love you the most," she said. Her hands grasped the mug, and then she slumped and fell to the ground.

Later, the emergency room doctor told me she had died before she hit the floor.

Goodbye, my beautiful Peggy Sue. I love you the most.

A MAN OF FEW WORDS

Suzanne Christie

The handsome young man with the piercing green eyes sitting next to me presses the gas pedal and the dilapidated VW rattles. It is October 9, 1965. We bust through the hills of Delaware heading for the Mason-Dixon Line. Next stop—the courthouse, Elkton, Maryland.

That is, if we can outrun and outfox my mother. The last thing the Protestant keep-up-appearances Evelyn Chubb wants is for me to marry the sexy, Camel-smoking, beer-drinking, Catholic hunk, David James Christie—a Temple medical student and ring man on the gymnastics team.

David is a man of few words, and he is hyperventilating when he approaches Reverend Sturgil. All he can say is, "We'd like to get married."

His large, strong hand shakes as he slips on the eleven-dollar gold ring on my hand. Later, I hear David ask Reverend Sturgil, "How much do I owe you?"

"It just depends on what it is worth to you."

I never knew how much David gave him but I think it was five dollars.

Our plan was to stay secretly married forever, but three weeks into my clandestine wedlock, my mother remarked on the phone, "Suzie, you do not sound like yourself. Did anything happen?"

I blurted out in my non-virgin voice, "I got married."

Evelyn screamed. "Get the train home Saturday and do not bring that guy. We will get this thing annulled."

My disappointed mother stayed angry for decades. And guess what? David didn't say a mean word to her the whole time. But there were times I would have liked him to be more talkative. Our honeymoon, for instance.

In my crazy passionate state of new love, I promised to go anywhere on our honeymoon and ended up on a road trip along the Alaskan highway. Our newlyweds' vacation was spent in a tent with me suffering from poison ivy and terrorized by the howl of nearby wolves. And eventually, too afraid to sleep outside, I curled up most nights on the bucket seat of our Dodge Dart. We were so broke when we hit Fairbanks that we had to get jobs at the Malemute Saloon for three weeks to have enough money to get home.

Focusing on the road, my quiet David barely spoke the whole trip. "I can't talk because I'm looking for a moose," he'd answer when I'd finally worked up enough nerve to ask what he was thinking.

My husband was a man of action and deeds . . . not words.

In 1970, David was awarded a Berry Deferment during the Vietnam War to complete his orthopedic residency. It was a shock when one hot June day he walked into our recently converted stone barn and threw down his little black bag and stethoscope.

"Sit down," he said. "I have something to tell you."

His father, Jimmy, a high school physics teacher, had just had a massive heart attack and I feared David was going to tell me my father-in-law had died. Instead, he announced he had called the Department of the Navy and relinquished his Berry Program Deferment. He didn't want to be an orthopedic surgeon tied to the hospital. His father's near-death experience made him realize that he wanted to be like his dad, a teacher who was home for dinner each night. He would be an emergency room doctor instead.

"Call them back and say you made a mistake!" I cried with a two-month-old Heather on my hip.

I wanted him to run to Canada. But my husband, a man of integrity with a military family tradition, believed the troops needed doctors. Two weeks later, he reported to Firebase Ross in Da Nang, Vietnam. We didn't speak on the farewell flight from Philadelphia to Los Angeles.

But every day he was gone, I ran to the mailbox to find a letter from him and every day, I wrote back. In the letters, he tells me he loves me over and over again (and what he wants to do to me under the feather tick).

I was one of the lucky ones. My soldier came home, and we defied every method of birth control—the pill, diaphragm, and IUD all failed and Jamie, Rich, and Tara were born, and joined their big sister Heather.

David never talked about the war, just saying that the rest of his life was gravy. Fifty-four years of marriage, four children, and eight grandchildren. The eleven old houses we restored. The stone walls and fountains he built. The paintings and drawings he created in his barn studio. The neighbors he stitched up in the ER. The sailboats he built with his sons. The nights he held me. And the many, many family dinners. All gravy.

David's been gone six years come February. He died in our eldest son, James' arms as I stood by his side. The irony is that this quiet man left me his beautiful words.

See, those letters we wrote back and forth to each other when he was in Vietnam? He saved them. After his death, I found a green suitcase in the eave of the attic filled with our love letters.

Dr. Seuss wrote, "Don't cry because it is over; smile because it happened."

I read our love notes over and over. And I smile despite my tears.

Stories are what make us human. What is your love story?

L@VE✉NOTES!

GO IN PEACE

Sam Baker & Liz Rose

Go in peace
Go in kindness
Go in love
Go in faith
Leave the day
The day behind us

Day is done
Go in grace
Let us go
Into the dark
Not afraid
Not alone
Let us hope
By some good pleasure

Safely to
Arrive at home

Let us hope
By some good pleasure

Safely to
Arrive at home

158

THAT'S IT FOLKS!

LOVENOTES!

Real Stories.

Real People.

Real Love.

XOXO,

Heather

THANK YOU FOR READING!

How To Get Involved &
Help Spread Love (and Hope)

LOVENOTES!
Real Stories, Real People, Real Love

1. Thanks for giving your reading time to LoveNotes! Which story resonated with you the most and why? Write to Heather at heather@ heatherchristiebooks.com with the subject line: **My Favorite Story**.

2. Tell your story with LoveNotes! Find details at www.Love-NotesWorldwide.com on how to . . .

    ♦ Audition for the annual New York City off-Broadway All-Star Show (held each February in Manhattan)

    ♦ Audition for one of the satellite city shows (Chicago, Indianapolis, and more coming soon)

    ♦ Submit your story for the next anthology

    ♦ Submit your story for the podcast (launching 2025)

3. Are you a creative entrepreneur or theater director? Launch a LoveNotes! satellite show in your community and become a member of the super cool LoveNotes! Producer's Mastermind Group. Select territories are being awarded now. Write to Heather at heather@heatherchristiebooks.com with the subject line: **LoveNotes! Producer Info.**

4. Attend a LoveNotes! show. Find links on how to purchase tickets to the All-Star off-Broadway New York City Show, plus the satellite city shows at www.LoveNotesWorldwide.com. A portion of ticket sales supports a local charity.

5. Need an inexpensive $15 date night? Watch the off-Broadway World Premiere of LoveNotes! on demand at https://www.heatherchristie-books.com/lovenotes-replay/

6. Follow the LoveNotes! Project on Facebook @heatherchristiebooks and @lovenotesworldwide and on Instagram @heatherchristiebooks and @lovenotes_worldwide and TikTok @heatherchristiebooks

7. If you loved this book (or liked it enough ;-)), write a five-star review on Amazon (even if you didn't buy it on Amazon) and Goodreads—this helps a little grassroots, independently published book like LoveNotes! gain traction among readers more than any other marketing technique. A sentence or two is perfect.

8. Ask your local library, bookstore, and gift store to carry LoveNotes! If they want special signed editions, have them write to Heather at heather@heatherchristiebooks.com.

9. Think of the LoveNotes! book when you need a present. Make it your next hostess gift. (It lasts a lot longer than a bottle of wine). And then there's Christmas, Hanukkah, Eid al-Fitr, Valentine's Day. Plus it would create a unique house-warming, wedding, anniversary, or even a bridesmaid's present.

10. Schedule an event with LoveNotes! creator Heather Christie. She is available for in-person and virtual gatherings: storytelling & writing workshops, class presentations, book clubs, speaking events, library

and bookstore appearances, panel discussions, and more! Send an email with your event idea to heather@heatherchristiebooks.com.

11. Sign up for Heather's newsletter to stay in the loop on all LoveNotes-y! developments, plus notifications about Heather's twice-yearly story-telling salon workshops in her Manhattan home, and more at www. HeatherChristieBooks.com or http://eepurl.com/bLM7D

ACKNOWLEDGMENTS

This book, and the idea for the entire LoveNotes! Project (the off-Broadway storytelling show, the satellite city shows, and the podcast) came to me during the loneliest, saddest, and darkest season of my life. It was by blind faith (and lots of therapy :-)) that I wrangled LoveNotes! into existence. I am humbled by and deeply grateful for this work.

I pulled a royal flush in the parent department, and that's why my first thank you always goes to my mother, Suzanne Christie, for her enthusiasm and slightly delusional belief that I can do anything. I miss my Dad. He's been gone for six years now. He was the first reader of my writing. I hope he knows I haven't given up. Thank you to my entire Christie Clan—James, Rich, Tara, your spouses, and your many offspring. And Aunt Susan—a theater usher who takes no bullshit.

Thank you to the Center at West Park, under the guidance of Debby Hirshman, for giving LoveNotes!, the storytelling show, a historic off-Broadway home. I am indebted to the inaugural LoveNotes! cast and book contributors—thank you for being my first. It was an honor to have Sam Baker share his voice and music in the world premiere. Thank you to John Edgar and Magda Bartkowska and the creative team at 71st Street Books.

Thank you to my dear and supportive friends: Sandy Barber, Haley Lawrence, Valerie Mackey, Teresa Bury, and the late Amy Rothermel. The list wouldn't be complete without Amy Impellizzeri, who has been my ride-or-die soul sister both in art and life.

Thank you to my healers: Christine Triano and Patrick Graves.

Thank you to my children—Cole Christie Snyder and Cali Christie Snyder—you make your goofball mom proud every day. Thanks for putting up with my creative shenanigans and giving my embarrassing Instagram posts a *like* once in a while.

Thank you to everyone who has shared his or her story with me. It takes courage to own our stories, and even more bravery to tell them.

Lastly, I am thankful for the darkness. Without it, I wouldn't know the light. I am grateful for it all. Here's to spreading love one story at a time. See you further on up the road.

Love,

Heather

ABOUT THE LOVENOTES! CREATOR/EDITOR

Heather Christie is a writer, producer, director, and educator. She is the winner of the National Indie Excellence Award for her novel, *What The Valley Knows* and its series companion, *The Lying Season.* Find her essays in Salon, Next Tribe, Writer's Digest, Baltimore Style, Scary Mommy, and Elephant Journal. She is the creator and producer of the Love-Notes! Real Stories. Real People. Real Love. storytelling show, book, and podcast, and the director of Listen To Your Mother NYC.

She holds an MFA in Creative Writing from Pine Manor College, and is an adjunct lecturer at the City University of New York.

Heather lives in New York City, but a piece of her heart remains in her small hometown near Reading, Pennsylvania. She loves to read, run, drink tea, make Sunday dinner, and she doesn't go anywhere without lipstick! Visit her website at www.HeatherChristieBooks.com.

LOVENOTES!
Contributors & Page Location

ANSWER KEYS

FIRST LOVE = A MAZE
Follow your heart!

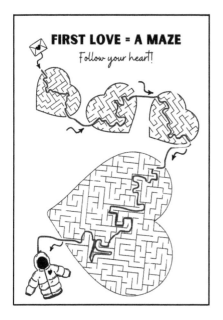

YOU NEVER KNOW WHERE YOU'LL FIND LOVE.
Locate the differences in the two pictures.

MAKE THIS HEART WHOLE.
Draw the other half.

WHEN L👀KING FOR LOVE . . .
Find these qualities!

TENDERNESS SMILES ENTHUSIASM LIKE HOPE
RESPECT DESIRE RISK HUMOR FUN FRIENDSHIP
KINDNESS AWE SAFETY INTEGRITY WANT
COMMUNICATION WARMTH HUGS KISSES WONDER

IT'S SAID THERE ARE AN EXTRAORDINARY AMOUNT OF FISH IN THE SEA. FIND THE 7 LOVENOTES! FISH

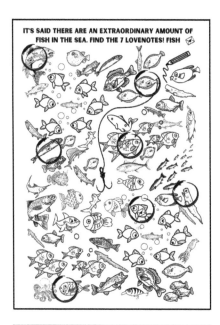

Love is sometimes a game of numbers!

FILL IN THE MISSING NUMBERS

1 + 1 = 💗

				21
9	5	0	10	24
8	5	4	6	23
9	2	0	0	11
5	8	4	5	22
31	20	8	21	19

- The missing numbers are integers between 0 and 10.
- The numbers in each row add up to totals to the right.
- The numbers in each column add up to totals along the bottom.
- The diagonal lines also add up to totals on the right.

EVERYBODY HAS A MATCH.

Find the Cupid couples.

NAME THE CODE & MESSAGE

.. / .-.. --- ...- . / .. .-.. --- ...- . ..-

Code: Morse Code   Message: I love you.

01001001 00100000 01101100 01101111
01110110 01100101 00100000 01111001
01101111 01110101

Code: Binary Code   Message: I love you.

143

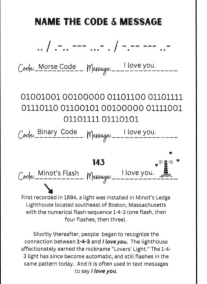

Code: Minot's Flash   Message: I love you.

First recorded in 1894, a light was installed in Minot's Ledge Lighthouse located southeast of Boston, Massachusetts with the numerical flash sequence 1-4-3 (one flash, then four flashes, then three).

Shortly thereafter, people began to recognize the connection between **1-4-3** and *I love you.* The lighthouse affectionately earned the nickname "Lovers' Light." The 1-4-3 light has since become automatic, and still flashes in the same pattern today. And it is often used in text messages to say *I love you.*

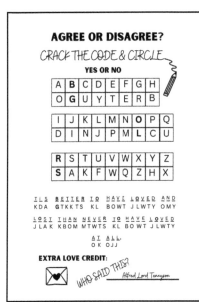

AGREE OR DISAGREE?

CRACK THE CODE & CIRCLE

YES OR NO

A	B	C	D	E	F	G	H
O	G	U	Y	T	E	R	B

I	J	K	L	M	N	O	P	Q
D	I	N	J	P	M	L	C	U

R	S	T	U	V	W	X	Y	Z
S	A	K	F	W	Q	Z	H	X

ILS BETTER TO HAVE LOVED AND
KDA GTKKTS KL BOWT JLWTY OMY

LOST THAN NEVER TO HAVE LOVED
JLAK KBOM MTWTS KL BO WT JLWTY

AT ALL.
OK OJJ

EXTRA LOVE CREDIT:

WHO SAID THIS? _Alfred Lord Tennyson_

Find words with four+ letters containing an
"O"

E C
R O N
A M

**THERE'S ONE LOVEY-DOVEY WORD THAT HAS ALL
7 LETTERS:** Romance

cremona, amorce, ancome, canoer, cornea, earcon,
enamer, macron, moaner, monera, acorn, cameo, canoe,
carom, caron, camae, corner, coram, crome, crone,
enorm, macon, macro, manor, maron, moner, morae,
morne, narco, norma, ocean, ocrea oncer, racon, recon,
roman, acro, aeon, aero, camo, cero, coma, come, cone,
core, corm, corn, eoan, mano, meno, moan, moer, mona,
mora, more, morn, noma, nome, norm omen, omer, once,
oner, orac, reno, roam, roan, roma, rone

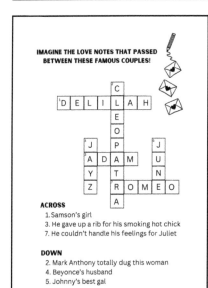

**IMAGINE THE LOVE NOTES THAT PASSED
BETWEEN THESE FAMOUS COUPLES!**

(crossword)
Across: 1. DELILAH, 3. ADAM, 7. ROMEO
Down: 2. CLEOPATRA, 4. JAYZ, 5. JUNE

ACROSS
1. Samson's girl
3. He gave up a rib for his smoking hot chick
7. He couldn't handle his feelings for Juliet

DOWN
2. Mark Anthony totally dug this woman
4. Beyonce's husband
5. Johnny's best gal

9 798991 704779